PRAISE FOR *SHOOT TO WIN*

"*Shoot to Win* is an in-depth primer that serves as a gateway to shooting success. Chris explores a variety of firearm platforms, examines the shooter mindset and provides readers useful knowledge that will help them get started on their journey into shooting." —Julie Golob, World Shooting Champion, author of *SHOOT: Your Guide to Shooting Competition*, and captain of Smith & Wesson's shooting team

"Chris's unique journey to the upper echelon of the competitive shooting world is fascinating. In *Shoot to Win*, Chris shares the secrets of his success and the insights on how he approaches his passion the way he does. It's a must read if you want to improve your skill set. Take this book to the range!" —Dana Loesch, host of the nationally syndicated radio show *The Dana Show*, host of *Dana* on The Blaze, television commentator

"Not only is he a shooting champion, Chris Cheng is an incredible inspiration. We've seen him on the hit television show *Top Shot*, but now we're hearing and learning from Chris first hand about how he won Season 4 after teaching himself how to shoot and compete. Through personal examples and a focus on basic fundamental techniques, Chris gives shooting beginners the confidence, motivation and knowledge they need to *Shoot to Win*." —Katie Pavlich, editor, *Townhall Magazine*, Fox News contributor

"The infectious enthusiasm Chris Cheng brings to shooting, and to life, explodes from the pages of *Shoot to Win*. Whether suggesting which gun to buy, how to get into competitive shooting, or drawing parallels between shooting and life, Chris delivers no-nonsense advice that will benefit anyone." —Tom Gresham, *Gun Talk Radio*

"Whether you're a new gun owner or a long time competitor, *Shoot To Win* is a fantastic book chock full of wisdom and expertise. As someone who spends more time in a studio than at a range, I found this book to be an invaluable addition to my training. —Cam Edwards, NRA News radio host of *Cam & Co.* on the Sportsman Channel

"Chris Cheng uncovers the 'top shot' in each of us. His book removes the barriers and allows the reader to discover the fun and responsibility of shooting, as well as owning, respecting, and securing firearms." —Rob Keck, Director of Conservation at Bass Pro Shops

"With *Shoot to Win*, Chris Cheng puts into words what so many of us understand but somehow rarely is discussed in a broader context. Shooting requires discipline of the body and mind, and those attributes translate into every other aspect of our lives. His advice and instruction is as relevant to the office or a classroom as it is to the range. Chris is a phenomenal ambassador for the firearms community, and *Shoot to Win* is a practical and inspirational place to start your journey into the world of firearms." —Natalie Foster, creator of GirlsGuidetoGuns.com, host of *Love at First Shot*, NRA News commentator

"Great insight into the world of shooting. An excellent read for people new to the sport." —Taran Butler, founder, Taran Tactical Innovations

"*Shoot to Win* is a thorough and fresh look at the fundamentals of firearms ownership and training that will benefit any gun owner." —Rob Pincus, owner, I.C.E. Training Company, Executive Director, Personal Defense Network

"Chris has been a great addition to the shooting world in recent years. Always happy and cheerful while at the same time being very dedicated and devoted to what he does . . . I wish him the best!" —Robert Vogel, World and National Champion Shooter, police and SWAT officer

SHOOT TO WIN

SHOOT TO WIN

Tips, Tactics, and Techniques to Help You
Shoot Like a Pro

Chris Cheng

Foreword by Dustin Ellermann

Afterword by Iain Harrison

Skyhorse Publishing

Skyhorse Publishing books may be purchased in bulk at special discounts for sales promotion, corporate gifts, fund-raising, or educational purposes. Special editions can also be created to specifications. For details, contact the Special Sales Department, Skyhorse Publishing, 307 West 36th Street, 11th Floor, New York, NY 10018 or info@skyhorsepublishing.com.

Skyhorse® and Skyhorse Publishing® are registered trademarks of Skyhorse Publishing, Inc.®, a Delaware corporation.

Top Shot®, HISTORY®, and their associated marks and logos are trademarks of A&E Networks, LLC.

Visit our website at www.skyhorsepublishing.com.

10 9 8 7 6 5 4 3 2

Library of Congress Cataloging-in-Publication Data is available on file.

Cover design by Owen Corrigan
Cover photo © Oleg Volk
On the cover: AR-15 style rifle by Houlding Precision Firearms. Scope by Leupold & Stevens: Mark 6 1-6x20 CMR-W. Ear protection by ESP America: Stealth model.

Print ISBN: 978-1-62873-699-1
Ebook ISBN: 978-1-62914-115-2

Printed in China

This book is dedicated to my parents, my sister, my friends, and my best *amigo*, Nate. Throughout the years they have always supported my fun and crazy ideas. I hope you have people in your life who encourage you to dream and think big.

I'd like to acknowledge the tremendous support I've received from *Top Shot*® alumni, who blazed the path that provided me the opportunity to be where I am today—living the American Dream.

Finally, my sponsor, Bass Pro Shops, has taken me in like family and I've seen how its founder, Johnny Morris, created such an amazing company.

TABLE OF CONTENTS

FOREWORD

Shooting has always been my favorite hobby and pastime. I'm not sure if I can really pin down the reason why I'm so attracted to the shooting sports, but while others have told me, "You'll grow out of it," I surely didn't; in fact, I only enjoy it more the older I get.

For a while I kept shooting as my "dirty little secret" because a loud minority in society tells us it's "politically incorrect." I even had family members who thought I was strange to be so passionate about sending lead downrange in a quick and precise manner. But I know that God gives us talents and abilities for a reason, and it was evident to see His plan come about through my experience in winning the third season of *Top Shot*.

Many youngsters in my part of the country start shooting firearms far earlier than I was allowed to. Except for a handful of occasions, I wasn't able to shoot anything but BB guns and archery until after I was sixteen years old. But, like Chris mentions in this book, the skills of pulling any trigger transfers to the real thing with the proper foundation. So those thousands of BBs that were shot by me as a youngster were slowly grooming me to be able to fire well-placed .50BMG rounds at moving targets 500 yards away and to hit golf balls with a .22 long rifle (.22LR) at 100 yards on a windy day.

Besides one defensive pistol course I took a few years back, I taught myself how to shoot. I can even remember discovering techniques as a youngster, such as rifle cant and trigger press with a Daisy BB gun, while shooting at my grandparents' farm. But in learning this way, by the seat of our pants, we sometimes teach ourselves wrong techniques. It is easier to learn to do something right the first time than to overcome a poor training scar after thousands of incorrect repetitions.

Proper training early on will help tremendously in your quest to become a better marksman. You are already starting off right by reading this book. And my advice on becoming a better shot is to simply focus on the fundamental techniques. To win *Top Shot*, we had to be able to adapt quickly to certain situations with any firearm or primitive weapon, but everything always boiled down to a smooth trigger press in the middle of intense pressure. Probably the best training I put myself through proceeding the competition was ripping the scope off of my Ruger 10/22, backing up to 115 yards, and keeping my balance while standing on top of a 5-inch fencepost and plinking steel downrange. It wasn't swinging upside down or flying through the air while shooting but just the simple focus of front sight and trigger press.

Whatever your goal is in becoming a skilled marksman, it is always enjoyable to shoot. So my final piece of advice is to just have fun with it and shoot straight!

—**Dustin Ellermann, *Top Shot* Season 3 Champion**

"Dustin may be the best shooter we ever had."

Those words spoken by *Top Shot* host Colby Donaldson echoed the sentiments of scores of viewers as they watched Dustin Ellermann shoot his way to the grand prize of season 3 of the HISTORY® network's top-rated program. And while his stunning performance at the final challenge stood the shooting world on its ear, it was Dustin's character that endeared so many to this twenty-eight-year-old from Zavalla, Texas. He brought no drama—only skill and passion along with a calm, cool demeanor—into shooting challenges that rattled the most seasoned competitors.

Before he was the *Top Shot* champion, Dustin was (and remains) the director of Camp His Way, a summer camp and year round retreat facility for Christian kids (www.camphisway.com). He and his wife are also foster parents and have three children of their own. And his easygoing attitude about shooting is much more impressive when you learn he was 99 percent self-taught.

"Shooting is fun to me, and I thank the Lord for the opportunity to be on *Top Shot* and to now be able to share my passion for shooting through clinics, range days, and other appearances," he says. "Putting God and family first, I look forward to seeing where this journey leads."

INTRODUCTION

Growing up in Orange County, California, I didn't have any friends whose parents owned guns. However, my Dad served in the US Navy, where he received some basic firearms training. After I was born, he purchased a Ruger Single Six .22 revolver and a Smith & Wesson Model 36 .38 Special revolver for home protection.

The author's first gun, which he shot at the age of six. A Ruger Single Six .22LR single-action revolver.

Like many Americans, I learned to shoot at the age of six under the tutelage of my father. I was a typical kid who loved playing with toy guns and anything that flung a projectile. Rubber bands, potatoes, marshmallows, BBs, pellets, water balloons, the oranges from the neighbor's tree—you name it, and me and my friends were trying to one up each other in games of marksmanship. I started developing my hand-eye coordination at a young age through these fun marksmanship games, along with many years of playing baseball and golf.

Shooting guns, however, was a very infrequent hobby. From ages six to thirty, I went to the range maybe twice every three to four years and rented a lane for an hour or two with my dad. However, during that time, I shot many other projectile devices, such as slingshots, BB guns, pellet guns, marshmallow guns, rubber-band guns, Super Soakers,

NERF guns, blow darts, water-balloon launchers, potato guns, and I'm sure many others I've since forgotten. During my training for *Top Shot*, l pulled on all of that hand-eye coordination experience.

My disposable income increased when I started working at Google at age twenty-seven, which allowed me to purchase my first gun. I opted for a SIG Sauer P226. Even though I'm a Glock guy now, SIGs will always hold a special place in my heart. Once I started watching the HISTORY network's *Top Shot* marksmanship competition, my interest in firearms was ignited. I was so energized by the excitement and fun of firearms that I decided to go out on a limb and apply for *Top Shot* Season 4.

So how did a self-taught amateur like me who had no military, law enforcement, or any formal training, and who only went to the range one hour a year, go on to win a nationally televised marksmanship competition?

I am excited to share with you the techniques I focused on and, just as important, my mentality and philosophy about winning—winning *Top Shot*, and winning in life.

This book is targeted toward beginning marksmen and markswomen who are looking to learn the basics. One thing I have learned is that there are so many schools of thought about firearms training, and so I do not claim that everything in this book will work for you. The best advice I can give is to learn as many techniques and forms as possible, and do whatever works best for you.

I hope to capture readers' other interests by layering on personal stories and anecdotes throughout my life that demonstrate how I've applied my skills in my personal and professional lives. I hope that my experiences and perspectives will help you win at life!

PART ONE:
SHOOT TO WIN—IN LIFE AND BEYOND

CHAPTER ONE

SETTING YOURSELF UP FOR SUCCESS

I'm staring down a line over 100 yards long, with seven tables full of guns and ammo. There are 150 people there to watch what's about to go down. All of a sudden, I hear someone yell "GO!" and I take off running. At the first table, I start loading a Kentucky Flintlock pistol and remind myself that trigger control is immensely important with this weapon. As I blow up two jugs, I move on to the 1860 Henry Repeating Rifle, where I focus on good cheek weld to make sure I get consistent hits. (Cheek weld is the idea of solidly placing your cheek in the optimal place on the comb.)

After taking down six metal rings, I run to a third table with a double-action Webley revolver. My job here is to shoot at a moving jar rack with nine targets. This whole time I am not alone. I have a fierce competitor trying to beat me, an Air Force veteran and federal police officer who is highly trained. He is right on my tail as we move through each station.

I run to the next station, where the Colt Peacemaker single-action revolver is waiting for me. I have to shoot two rows of steel plates down without missing. I had fallen short on this exact challenge a few weeks earlier, and I knew I had to *stay focused with a positive, winning attitude.*

I had a perfect run, but so did my competition, and we headed into a fifth station with a crossbow. With three moving targets to hit,

I took aim through the optical scope and got a shotgun-type lead to make sure I got solid hits. My competition got two beats ahead of me as we moved into the sixth station, a fully automatic machine gun, the M1919. Here again I knew that trigger control was going to be important so that I could control my sight picture through the iron sights. As we exploded our targets 100 and 125 yards down range, I was still a beat or two behind at the final station, a Milkor M32A1 grenade launcher.

The author's view of the final stage on *Top Shot* Season 4, using the Milkor M32A1 grenade launcher. Photo courtesy of HISTORY.

I had never fired a grenade launcher in my life, and here I am competing against the 2003 World Grenadier Champion. Not only that, I am behind. The writing may have been on the wall, but I have never been one to give up without a fight.

I believed that I could win. I had visualized myself getting to this point and pulling it off. My competitor blew up his first platform and was already working on his second and final platform before I even got my first shot off. I brought up the grenade launcher and looked through the scope, acquired a solid sight picture of both targets, and started ripping off rounds.

The next thing I knew, my platforms had exploded and that was it.

I had just claimed the title of *Top Shot* champion, a $100,000 grand prize, and a professional marksmanship contract with Bass Pro Shops.

Just six weeks prior to this, I was working my day job at Google behind a computer eight to ten hours a day, and now all of a sudden my entire life had just changed. Throughout this book I introduce firearms and sports psychology concepts I focused on to build my marksmanship skills, and maintain a fierce, competitive edge. I imagine you may be unfamiliar with many of these concepts, but by the end of this book we will have gone into detail about all of them.

I'm excited to share my experience going from self-taught amateur to professional marksman. What were the techniques and mechanics I focused on? How did I train? What kind of mental exercises did I go through to help me beat seventeen other experienced competitors? A lot of what I hope to share is how I drew on my other life experiences. I've inserted anecdotes throughout the book to draw connections between baseball, work, music, and firearms. I've always taken a holistic view of my skills and capabilities when tackling a problem at hand, and I hope it's a concept you will find insightful and useful in your own life.

Before diving into any of the technical and training pieces around shooting, I'd like to share how I approach most things in my life, including shooting. It's a key part of how I approach marksmanship and the training, communication, and discipline that comes with it. A framework that drastically affected my perspective was teaching Googlers how to create a Personal Development Plan (PDP). Google, along with many other companies worldwide, use the PDP framework. After delivering many PDP training sessions over the course of my last year at Google, I became a huge fan of this skills-perspective framework.

A PDP boils down to answering the following questions:
- What skills do you currently have?
- What skills do you want to have?
- Which skills are you using at work and play?
- What are your short-term goals?
- What are your long-term goals?
- What is preventing you from achieving these goals?
- What people, groups, mentors, or other people can you rely on to help you achieve those goals?
- Why do you enjoy using these skills?

The way someone organizes their PDP is up to the individual. Some people put it in a document, others in a PowerPoint presentation—I put mine in a Google Spreadsheet, which I have made available at (http://goo.gl/avQhqV). Note that this was last updated in 2011, right before I left to compete on *Top Shot*, so my career goals were very different at the time.

I wanted to go to business school and creating my own tech start-up. While the business school ship has sailed, I do still harbor this dream.

A Note on Failure

You aren't pushing your boundaries unless you sometimes fail. I tried to get into a Top 10 business school for two years and could only manage to get waitlisted, but not accepted, twice. While perseverance is a fantastic trait, sometimes you need to know when to change course. Part of what I think has made me successful is knowing when to pivot and take advantage of a better opportunity that either comes along, or that I create. For me, the opportunity that was better than business school was pursuing my professional marksmanship contract with Bass Pro Shops. I wanted to explore a completely new industry and see how much fun I could have.

To really put things into perspective, had I gotten into business school, I may not have been able to take six weeks off to compete in *Top Shot*. My whole life trajectory changed for the better, as a result of a failure.

I look at failure as an opportunity to learn and prevent that failure from happening again. Sometimes failure opens up other doors, and you just have to be patient. Whatever the reason, I have never let any of my failures slow me down in life. I hope you don't either.

You can note skills you have from your personal life in your PDP, so it's not all business. Perhaps you play poker like I do, where a few of the related skills are concentration, risk-taking, and statistical analysis. Or perhaps you have children and are a good multitasker and time organizer, with all the tasks and responsibilities that come with raising kids. With marksmanship, some related skills are an ability to stay focused and follow instructions, and to be mind/body aware. Thinking about all of your skills and your current competency— whether you want to improve, or whether you can ditch a skill set— are important so you know where to focus your time and energy. Including personal skills will enable you to see a fuller picture of your capabilities, and, who knows, perhaps enable you to make a career out of your hobby.

While there's a bit more to a PDP, the essence of the structure and approach is to think about the aforementioned questions and to put your answers down on paper. Having the words down on paper can help make things more tangible, and also makes it easier to share your hopes and dreams with your colleagues, friends, and family who are interested in helping.

I think a big key to unlocking one's success is to first know thyself, so well that you can explain who you are to someone else—be it a recruiter, your friends, your family, etc. This includes your weaknesses and blind spots. Being honest about our shortcomings can be very challenging for a lot of people, myself included. Here's an exact copy of what I used to discuss with newly hired Googlers who I used to manage:

The Chris Cheng Owner's Manual

This guide will provide instructions on how to work best with Chris. If there's anything faulty with Chris, please do not mail him in for repair. Just tell him directly.

Chris's Management Philosophy and Style

Maximizing Happiness	My primary goal is to maximize your happiness. As your manager, I want to help make your job a key contributor to your personal/professional happiness.
You're the maestro	I spent my former days playing double bass in orchestra and jazz band, and the idea here is that as your manager, I'm not the maestro, you are. You're in charge of telling me what you want to do, what you want to achieve, and how you think you can best go about doing it. I'm your biggest fan who will help identify and open up the opportunities on the team that will help you get to where you want to go.
Empowering you!	If you come to me with a question/problem, my goal is to help empower you with the answer. What this means is that I may ask your question right back to you (so what do you think is the best solution for X?), and ask additional probing questions to help you find the answer. I truly believe that empowerment happens when the individual discovers things for themselves (with/without the help of others), as opposed to something being dictated/directed from above.

Focus on big picture career stuff	Why are you here? What is your higher purpose? What are your hopes and dreams for your career? What do you want to achieve, and how do you need my help? I think it's really easy to get lost in the day-to-day work, and I like helping you keep an eye on the prize through meaningful career discussions.
Diplomacy	I have Political Science and International Relations degrees, which leads to my desire to be diplomatic. I like to think that I can deliver hard feedback in a nice way, but if you end up thinking I'm being too soft, you may need to call me out on this. I sometimes fear that being too blunt will hurt feelings, but I can definitely adapt to the person or situation, so just let me know.
Personality type	MBTI and True Colors are languages I enjoy. I'm an ENTP and Orange/Blue. I think it's helpful to have conversations around what this means for us.
Concision	I really appreciate short and concise communication, whether it's an email, face-to-face conversation, or other medium. If you ramble on for too long, I am still listening to you and I'll be burning a lot of energy to focus, which can wear me out. Focus on the main points, think bullet points, and we'll be fine :)
RELAX (Be Type B)	I consider myself to be outgoing, friendly, and funny. I guess I have what they call a "big personality." I'm aware that this can be intimidating. However, if you are in any way intimidated, that's not my intent, and just tell me how you want me to interact differently with you.
Be on time (Be Type A)	OK, conflicts with the above, but I hate tardiness, it's part of my Type A personality. My father was a salesman and a military officer in the U.S. Navy, where punctuality is expected. Growing up, we had family dinner at 6PM on the dot, every single weekday. "On time is late, 5 minutes early is on time" runs constantly throughout my head. You may see this Type A & B interplay at various times :)

Skillz, skillz, skillz	One of my previous managers opened my eyes to viewing career development through skill development. I like to focus on your personal/professional growth, and identify opportunities to develop your skills. Let's hone in on the core set of skills you need to accomplish your career goals, then find those opportunities where you can flex your skills!

Things to note here are how I discuss my goals, my intentions, and management and communication style with the hope of improving communication with my direct reports. I also insert a lot of personal hobbies as context, which were oftentimes fun points of discussion. Whenever my interest in marksmanship would come up, even here in liberal Silicon Valley, I often received interested responses from colleagues who would say that they've been meaning to go try shooting but either didn't know anyone or didn't know how to get started. In a management context, I always thought it helped to know my colleagues on a personal level and engage them in social activities outside of work.

Understand my career goals, and what motivates me	I make decisions based on how well something aligns with the big picture. I am driven by things that make a difference in the world, and being a change-maker is another thing that drives me.
Clear the deck	Shield me from extraneous noise and other distractions. Help me focus on the high priority items, and clear the path for success.
Challenge me	I like a manager who will challenge me to go above and beyond. While I'm very self-motivated, I tend to focus on my strong areas such as people and project management, and at times I could use a little prodding to focus on my weaker areas, such as data analysis.

Laissez-Faire	I prefer my manager take a hands-off approach, and provide me with the right level of guidance and support to help me succeed in my tasks. I am very proactive in communicating what I'm doing, whether it be through email updates, IMs, in person chats, etc, so I will be pushing a fair amount of info your way.
Inspire me	Get me excited about the work. It will go a long way.
Be Direct and Transparent	If there's a problem with something I'm doing, I want to know about it and expect my manager will be direct and timely with this feedback. I hate B.S.—just tell me whatever needs to be said. I am not a delicate flower.

You'll also note a section on how I like to be managed, which I would discuss with my manager to make sure we were on the same page. Since we're all dynamic people who can change over time, I'd like to emphasize that I viewed this document as a dynamic resource, like my PDP, that could change over time. In fact, it should change as I continue to learn new ways of doing things and take on bigger responsibilities.

A sidebar here is how I came about the idea of an "owner's manual." Google is the type of company that encourages openness and the sharing of information within the company. If I wanted to know what was going on in a different team, even if I had no business need to know, the culture was such that most Googlers would share as much information as they could. The Google intranet is built on Google Sites and Google Docs, which is easily searchable. I came upon the owner's manual of Urs Hölzle, a Google Senior Vice President, through his internally shared Google Doc. Since imitation is the greatest form of flattery, I decided to flatter Urs and make my own version.

On the topic of openness, I have seen a very strong parallel between Google culture and firearm culture, where the exchange of information happens at a furious pace. If I'm at the range and need some help, I can ask anyone I need for a tool, advice, or really anything. On the web, gun geeks exchange all sorts of information, including tips and tricks, and it was this huge source of information that helped me train for *Top Shot*. I still use the web (read: Google) to find useful firearm information every day.

Back to the PDP, for certain skills I just started small, such as accepting that I am not naturally gifted at basketball. But it goes a bit deeper than that. At times, I don't like doing things I'm not good at, sometimes for fear that I'm going to look stupid, other times because I don't want to look incompetent. So, knowing this about my personality, sometimes I have to push myself to try a new activity, and push on even if I'm not very good at it.

Beyond knowing our strengths and weaknesses, we bring our full selves to the task at hand when we can use our entire skill set at any given moment.

Under the Gun

On *Top Shot* Season 4, I ended up going into an elimination challenge against William, an FBI Special Agent who spent eleven years on the US Marine Corps Shooting Team as both a shooter and coach. We were shooting the 1860 Henry Repeating Rifle at five sets of three concentric metal rings; first man to knock down all his targets wins. There's nothing quite like the excitement, and stress, of a head-to-head challenge. While neither one of us had ever competed with the Henry rifle before, William had more than a decade of rifle experience, compared with my occasional visit to the range with my AR-15. I knew going against William was going to be challenging, to say the least.

About two-thirds of the way in the challenge, I was behind— really behind. I had only six of the fifteen targets down, compared with William's eleven. When the host, Colby Donaldson, noted that I was behind and that I had to "pick up the pace," I felt that stress. But when that happened, I thought about previous times at work, when planning events, and other situations where I had felt similar stress. I know that, for my body, stress actually helps me focus and perform at a higher level. That burst of stress was the turning point in the challenge: I started building momentum, it came down to the wire, and I eventually won.

One of my skills is knowing how to handle pressure, and it's a skill I can apply in competition, at work, and in other life situations. This is one example where I tapped my skill set from past experiences and applied it to an active situation. And, of course, the next time I'm stressed out, I can rely on this *Top Shot* example of how I struggled but also came from behind to win.

As I noted earlier, the last time I updated my PDP was 2011. Since winning *Top Shot*, I have spent that time exploring a new industry, getting an understanding of the lay of the land, trying to find my place, and where I want to go with this new career path. I didn't know anyone in the firearms industry and so I started from square one. It's probably about time that I revisit my PDP and update my skill set, and redefine what my short and medium-term goals are. My long-term goal is still the same, running for some sort of public office. We'll see if the right opportunity presents itself over the next decade.

For me, there's a balance between being a jack of all trades and a master of a specific skill. While some situations may call for you to be a master of a particular skill, at other times you may need to be simply competent enough in a variety of skills. For *Top Shot*, I think the fact that I didn't have any formal training gave me a fairly big advantage. I was a jack of all trades who was very open to learning new techniques, so my viewpoint during *Top Shot* practice sessions was from a fairly clean slate. I didn't have years of training getting in my way of learning something new. Many marksmen spend years learning a specific weapon and technique, and then they get locked into what they know.

On the other hand, there are times that require you to completely master a skill. The following is one example:

Point of Order

I helped restart my fraternity chapter at the University of California, Los Angeles in 1998. Sigma Alpha Epsilon had been off campus for about five years, and it was time for us to return. I was an executive officer for my chapter, and part of my duties was being the parliamentarian. As a nineteen-year-old, I had no idea what *Robert's Rules of Order* was and neither did most of my fraternity brothers.

Our weekly chapter meetings were so terribly run and disorganized that it drove me to find out how we could improve things. I studied *Robert's Rules of Order* like nobody's business. Within a week, I took the unofficial role of parliamentarian by announcing in a meeting that we were going to uphold our bylaws and use parliamentary procedure. I had to know the rules inside and out, and occasionally there was a challenge to the rules where I had to render the final verdict in a confident, authoritative way. There is little room for error in parliamentary procedure, and I did not want to make any mistakes for the sake of being fair to my brothers, and to honor the process.

Our meetings started to run more efficiently and more orderly, where we actually had great discussions and voted on pressing matters. Many brothers would occasionally moan and groan when I would inject parliamentary procedure into the discussion, but I think, or at least hope, that in the end everyone appreciated the structure. Any of my fraternity brothers reading this right now are either rolling their eyes, or chuckling to themselves.

To tie this all together, before I even get involved in an activity I ask myself, How does this fit into a goal I have for myself? Then I ask, How do I get there, who can help me, and who or what is going to get in my way? Once I'm actively involved in a situation at work or elsewhere, I tap into my entire skill set to help me accomplish the task.

At work, instead of being focused on skills, I used to be more focused on titles, where the goal was to get promoted and get a better title. But oftentimes, in the chase to get promoted, you end up developing skills that you may not enjoy or may not need, but that are required to move up the ladder. The secret sauce I think we're all looking for is finding the job where we use and develop the skills we want to focus on and enjoy using. This will naturally lead to higher performance, and then the promotion naturally comes through that progression. Aren't we more likely to do a great job if we really enjoy what we're doing?

And this leads us to the final question in the list at the start of this chapter: why do you like using a particular skill? With marksmanship, I hope that you'll get a better understanding of why you want to learn how to shoot, and of how to leverage all your skills to learn how to shoot to the best of your ability. We'll explore the answer to that question in chapter 4, "Why Learn to Shoot?"

Chapter Summary

- Believe you can win. It doesn't matter whether this is at work, play, or home. If you don't believe in yourself, then you will probably fail.
- Create a life framework, such as your own Personal Development Plan (PDP).
- Push yourself. Fail, and fail hard. You aren't pushing yourself hard unless you occasionally fail hard. The key is to learn from your mistakes so you can be successful in the future.
- Know your strengths, weaknesses, and blind spots.
- Know how everything you are doing fits into the bigger picture.

CHAPTER TWO

THE FOUR RULES OF FIREARMS SAFETY

The following Four Rules of Firearms Safety must be abided by at all times. This is not just for your own safety, but for the safety of others around you.

1. Treat all guns as if they are loaded.
2. Never cover the muzzle with anything you are not willing to destroy.
3. Keep your finger off the trigger until you're ready to fire.
4. Be sure of your target and what is beyond it.

There are variants of these rules, so let's review the salient points.

1. Treat all guns as if they are loaded

This might sound silly to someone new to firearms, since you might think "well, it's easy to know when a gun is loaded or not." I've heard too many stories of carelessness, many from seasoned professionals. Here's one such story:

Death of the Yellow Pages

As if the Internet hadn't already accomplished this, a SWAT commander friend of mine helped move it along. He was home one evening watching TV, performing dry-fire (firing without ammunition) practice drills with his pistol and empty magazines. As his target, he had a thick yellow-pages phone book standing up next to the TV. While watching his favorite show, he was going through his normal dry-fire practice routine: acquiring a good sight picture, aligning his sights, slowly squeezing the trigger, trapping the trigger, racking the action, and resetting.

He was also practicing his reloading technique with empty magazines. After the reset, he would grab a magazine from the pile of six or seven mags sitting in a bowl next to him. He had done this practice routine for years, going through the motions thousands and thousands of times without any problem. While engrossed in his TV show, he remembered taking aim at the phone book, squeezing the trigger, and getting the surprise of his life. BOOM! The phone book fell, and his wife and kids started screaming down the stairs to see if he was alright.

Luckily, the phone book was the only thing that sustained any damage (the bullet went about two-thirds of the way through) and no one was injured. To this day, he still doesn't know how a live round got into one of the magazines that he was 100 percent sure were empty and clear.

The lesson learned here is that you must triple-check your weapon to make sure it is unloaded. More on this in later chapters.

2. Never cover the muzzle with anything you are not willing to destroy

The muzzle is the end of the gun where the bullet exits. Whatever is in front of a muzzle while a gun is discharged will be destroyed. All guns are deadly weapons that should be treated with respect. As a range officer, I have seen lots of careless mistakes made by casual and competition shooters alike. I've seen casual shooters at the range turn around 180 degrees, with their back to the firing line, holding a loaded gun to get their picture taken with their buddy. In their attempt to look cool while posing with a gun, they are also pointing their gun straight at some innocent person. To make matters worse, their finger is on the trigger.

As a range officer, I've learned to never assume that everyone knows and follows the four safety rules. I will give people the benefit of the doubt when I intervene to help correct the matter, but pretty much all ranges will ban repeat rule offenders. Everyone at the range wants to have fun in a safe atmosphere, and 99.99 percent of the time there aren't any problems.

For competition shooters, I've seen shooters run to the next target array and "sweep" their hand or arm in front of the muzzle.

The National Rifle Association's (NRA's) first fundamental rule for safe gun handling that correlates to point 2 is "ALWAYS keep the gun pointed in a safe direction." This golden rule is the most important. The thought process here is that, even if a shooter forgets or does not follow the other safety rules, as long as the gun is pointed in a safe direction no one would get injured.

You might be asking, "What is a safe direction?" If you're at a range, the safe direction is downrange toward where everyone is shooting their targets. There's typically a straight line that shooters should stay behind, shooting perpendicular to this line in one direction.

Generally speaking, it's easier to control the muzzle on long guns, such as a rifle or shotgun, compared with a pistol, which has a shorter barrel. While practicing or competing, you'll need to develop a strong muzzle awareness of not only the gun you are shooting but of the other guns that may be in your vicinity.

3. Keep your finger off the trigger until you're ready to fire

The trigger finger is clearly off the trigger and resting on the side of the frame. The trigger finger can be even higher if it is the shooter's preference.

The picture above is one you should memorize. Whether you're holding a pistol, rifle, or shotgun, your finger should be off the trigger and outside of the trigger guard until you are ready to fire. Many new shooters have a hard time putting this rule into practice. I had some difficulties when I first got into competition shooting, where a few range officers were pointing out to me that I had my finger on the trigger during reloads, when I was moving with my pistol, or otherwise not ready to fire. As with anything, practice makes perfect.

A Potentially Deadly Mistake

Once I was a student at a defensive pistol-training course where we had sixteen students whose skills ranged from newbie to professional. We were on the firing line practicing live-fire drills under the supervision of multiple teachers. Our instructors initiated a jam-clearing drill in which we had to reload with a fresh magazine and rack the action, or pull back the slide to chamber the first round. A student just six feet from me racked the action, but inadvertently had her finger on the trigger. When the slide went forward she accidentally pulled the trigger and sent a round flying, startling herself, me, the instructors, and other students.

Even though she wasn't following rule 3, she was following rule 2 and had her muzzle pointed downrange in a safe direction, so no one was injured.

This is another safety rule that must not just be memorized but also ingrained in your muscle memory.

4. Be sure of your target and what is beyond it

Even once you've confirmed your target, you also need to consider what is beyond it. Are you shooting into a backstop or a large hill that can stop the type of ammunition you're using? If you are indoors, do you know what is above and below you?

Before firing, make sure you are 100 percent sure of your target and your surroundings.

I'm normally not one to make absolute statements, but there is simply no compromise with safety and firearms. If you can't or don't want to abide by these safety rules, then don't bother learning how to shoot. I won't want to shoot with you, nor will other responsible people.

Additional Considerations

In addition to the four rules of firearm safety, there are other safety issues that should be considered.

Ear and Eye Protection

Ear Protection

Vision and hearing are critical senses we want to protect while participating in firearms-related activities. As a point of reference, the US Department of Labor Occupational Safety & Health Administration (OSHA) requires that, in the workplace, if "any employee's [noise] exposure may equal or exceed an 8-hour time-weighted average of 85 decibels, the employer shall develop and implement a monitoring program."

While most of us won't be shooting over an eight-hour period, the 85-decibel guideline is one piece we can use on as a baseline.

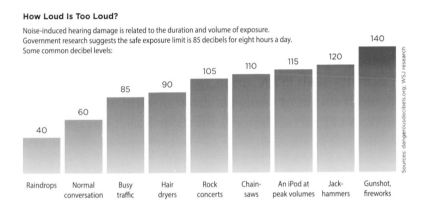

How Loud Is Too Loud?
Noise-induced hearing damage is related to the duration and volume of exposure. Government research suggests the safe exposure limit is 85 decibels for eight hours a day. Some common decibel levels:

40 Raindrops
60 Normal conversation
85 Busy traffic
90 Hair dryers
105 Rock concerts
110 Chain-saws
115 An iPod at peak volumes
120 Jack-hammers
140 Gunshot, fireworks

Sources: dangerousdecibels.org; WSJ research

Gunshots are way above OSHA's safe-exposure limit of 85 decibels, so you'll want to make sure to take care of your hearing.

Ear protection options vary widely. On the low end of the cost scale, foam plugs can often work fine, but I recommend in-ear foam or rubber plugs such as those offered by SureFire. These are comfortable and, more important, effective.

Earmuffs are another option to consider. Earmuffs completely cover your ears and provide very good protection. There are many affordable options for these as well. The downside to earmuffs is that they can get very sweaty and uncomfortable if you wear them for long periods of time. It's also hard to hear conversations with earmuffs, and, if you're receiving instruction from someone, you'll want to be able to clearly hear what your instructor is saying.

There are also many electronically amplified earmuffs. This type of protection will cut the amplification when the external sound level is at a dangerous level. Electronic muffs are nice in that you can clearly hear conversations even through gunfire. Note that performance indoors may be affected because of the acoustics.

On the high end of the cost scale, there are custom-fit plugs.

Cheap foam plugs, affordable SureFire EP7 plugs, and high-end electronic noise-cancelling plugs, custom fit by ESP America.

I highly recommend plugs from Electronic Shooters Protection (aka ESP America). I use them exclusively while at the range and in competition. My ESPs are great because they enable me to hear normal talking while cancelling out loud noises, such as gunshots. Because they are custom fit, they don't make my ears sweat or otherwise cause discomfort. I have literally worn them for six hours at a time when out at competitions and other shooting events. While custom plugs can be pricey, you get what you pay for. Since I'm also a musician, I can't afford to have anything happen to my hearing.

To get custom plugs made, you'll need to schedule an appointment with your local audiologist so they can create molds of your ear canals. They'll send them to ESP, and within two weeks you'll have your custom plugs. They use readily available batteries that are common in standard hearing aids.

When choosing your ear protection, you'll need to consider the following:

- What type of weapon you will be shooting. With pistols, all options are fine. However, with shotguns and rifles, if you are wearing earmuffs it's possible that you may not get a good cheek weld, the buttstock of the long gun may push the earmuffs off, or both.
- What caliber you will be shooting. This comes down to personal preference as to whether muffs or plugs will work best. You might need to try some different brands and styles before you find ear protection that works for the particular caliber you're shooting. For .22LR or rounds of a similar caliber, simple foam plugs will suffice. On the opposite end of the spectrum, with .223 rifle rounds or larger, or with shotgun rounds, many shooters opt to double up and use both plugs and muffs. It just depends on your ears' sensitivity.

Eye Protection

If you wear prescription glasses, it's fine to wear them to protect your eyes when you're shooting. However, I would suggest purchasing a pair of specialized shooting glasses, since they are often designed to wrap around your eyes to protect them from shrapnel and fragments that are commonplace at ranges.

While regular sunglasses may also work, I would suggest purchasing a pair of ANSI-rated glasses. Companies like Rudy Project, ESS, and Oakley have fantastic products, many of which also have interchangeable lenses that help you adapt to many lighting environments.

Read the Owner's Manual

I can understand if you don't like reading the manual for the fancy tech gadget you just bought, or for that new IKEA cabinet that's now missing a wood dowel or three. However, every firearm make and model is unique, and the instruction manual has useful information about the gun's parts and how they work, how to load and unload the gun, the location of the safety—if there even is one—and repair and warranty information.

I read every instruction manual for each of the guns I acquire to make sure I am 100 percent confident I know how to operate that particular firearm safely.

Keep Your Gun Clean and Functional

Guns are mechanical tools that need to be cared for, cleaned, and maintained if they are to have a long life and be safe to operate. We'll review cleaning in chapter 20, but if anything on your gun appears to stop working, you should take the gun to a qualified gunsmith.

If you decide to compete, then having a clean gun is essential to success. A jam or malfunction during a match can ruin your chance of doing well. Clean guns are more accurate as well; fouling and other gunk in the barrel can greatly affect a bullet's trajectory.

Ideally, you should clean your gun after each use, but This isn't always possible or necessary if you only shoot a few rounds before safely storing your firearm. The type of ammunition, as well as environmental conditions, can affect how dirty your firearm gets. For beginners, I recommend cleaning your firearm after each time you use it, no matter how many rounds you put through it. It is good practice to learn how to properly clean and maintain your firearm, and cleaning it will also help you learn the mechanics more intimately.

Prevent Unauthorized Access to Your Guns

It should come as no surprise that the single person responsible for the security of a firearm is the owner. Specifically, children should not have access any firearms unless they are properly supervised by a knowledgeable adult. Preventing accidents and theft can be achieved by securely storing your firearms. We'll review specifics in the next chapter.

Chapter Summary:

- The Four Rules of Firearms Safety:
  1. Treat all guns as if they are loaded.
  2. Never cover the muzzle with anything you are not willing to destroy.
  3. Keep your finger off the trigger until you're ready to fire.
  4. Be sure of your target and what is beyond it.
- Wear eye and ear protection.
- Read the owner's manual.
- Keep your gun clean.
- Prevent unauthorized access to your guns.

CHAPTER THREE

SAFELY STORING YOUR FIREARM

As a gun owner, you are completely responsible for securing your gun, making sure only authorized persons have access to it. If you have young children, it is particularly important to keep your firearm secured when not in use under adult supervision. Securing your firearm is also necessary to prevent potential thieves—who may in turn use it against an innocent person. You should also check your local and state laws, which actually may require certain types of firearm security in your home. Your local police department or gun shop should know the details.

One home defense consideration is the trade-off between speed and security. A highly secured firearm may not be easy to retrieve quickly. Another consideration is concealing your secured firearms to make it harder for unauthorized persons to locate them. This could mean putting your gun safe in a closet, under a bed, behind a cabinet in a hollow wall, or other concealed location.

There is no shortage of gun storage and safety options.

Storage and Safety Options

Trigger Lock

I used to have cable locks with keys (see below) on all my guns, but then I had to worry about losing the keys and keeping track of which key went to which lock. Now I prefer Master Lock's cableless trigger locks that use simple combination codes instead of keys. I only have to remember my combination code—and I don't have to worry about securing keys, either. Master Lock trigger locks will not scratch or mar your gun's trigger or the surrounding area, and they are very affordable. I secure all my guns with them.

A gun trigger lock, #94DSPT by MasterLock.

Cable Lock

A gun cable lock, #107DPST by MasterLock.

This type of lock loops through an open action and are locked by either key or combination.

Gun Vault or Safe

These come in many shapes and sizes, and locking mechanisms include key, biometric (mostly fingerprint), and combination dial or code. They can hold anywhere from one pistol to twenty to thirty pistols and long guns and beyond. Securing the safe to the ground, wall, or other immovable surface is advisable to keep a thief from running off with the safe.

Soft Case

Soft cases are nice because they are generally lighter and more compact than hard cases. Many types are available, and the price is usually lower for soft cases as well. Some soft cases can be slim, where you basically can only fit the weapon, but others have pockets and more room for ammo, magazines, and other accessories.

Hard Case

There are also many hard cases available. Some popular brands include Pelican and SKB. While hard cases are heavier, they are naturally more secure and can protect your guns from harsher impacts. If you ever fly with guns, you have to have a hard case. Let's not forgot that you also need some quality locks to protect your investment. For my hard cases, I also use Master Lock, as it has affordable, high-quality locks. I also recommend combination locks on cases so you don't have to manage all the keys.

I prefer to store my guns with the actions open as an extra safety precaution that demonstrates to me, and others, that the gun is not ready to fire. Note that an open action alone does not guarantee the gun is not loaded. This is why, when clearing a firearm, you should always visually and physically check the chamber to confirm the gun is unloaded. The safe handling of firearms cannot be overemphasized.

I also recommend storing your guns and ammunition in separate locations. This is simply a safety redundancy in the event an unauthorized person, especially a child, gets access to your gun. With the ammunition stored in a separate place, you are creating an environment that makes an accidental discharge more difficult.

For a monthly fee, certain gun ranges rent out lockers, storage space, or both for your firearms. Check with your local gun ranges and clubs.

A final consideration for firearms storage is humidity. Humidity is bad for firearms, causing rust and other damage. Storing a dehumidifier or dehumidifier crystals with your firearm can greatly reduce the humidity and extend its life.

Chapter Summary:

- There are many firearm security and safety options, including trigger locks, cable locks, gun safes, and hard and soft cases.

CHAPTER FOUR

WHY LEARN TO SHOOT?

Before going into any of the technical aspects of marksmanship, I think it's important to ask yourself, "*Why* am I interested in learning how to shoot?" Your answer will be your motivation and give you a direction for your training. And your reasons may change over time. I originally started for fun, but my appreciation and interest in shooting has expanded far beyond fun.

Below are a number of reasons, and this is by no means an exhaustive list.

For Fun

Going to the range can be a great way to unwind and have some fun with your friends, family, and loved ones.

If you want to shoot just for fun, you might want to consider going the self-taught route like I did and read books and articles online, and watch all the YouTube videos that are available on this topic. The awesomeness of the Internet comes through for us once again.

Geeks for Guns

The Silicon Valley folks I interacted with during my time at Google mostly had a neutral to positive interest in shooting guns. Like many people, they had seen them on TV and in the movies and had a healthy fear and respect of guns.

I was often the person on my team who arranged for fun team off-sites, and one quarter I organized a trip to our local gun range near Google headquarters in Mountain View, California. Once at the range, the twelve of us went through a safety meeting in a training room, where we reviewed the four safety rules. We headed into the shooting bays with a mixture of pistols and a Remington 870 12-gauge pump shotgun. Some of the range employees were on hand to help manage our group.

I distinctly remember the smiles of joy and excitement as I watched many of my colleagues shoot a firearm for the first time. Naturally, some of them struggled, but many of them were also excellent shots. For high-tech people who spend all day staring at a computer or phone screen, a low-tech activity such as shooting guns can be a very pleasurable experience. Some companies, even have shooting groups, such as the Adobe Shooters League and the QShooters Club, where the company pays for recreational shooting activities.

Google has its own internal mailing list for Googler gun folks where casual group trips to the range, tech specs around guns, ammo, and gear are all vigorously discussed and scrutinized.

Tech people naturally love technical things, and so there is a natural attraction for tech geeks and gun geeks.

Training for *Top Shot*

When I applied for *Top Shot* Season 4, I trained for five months, putting in twenty to twenty-five hours per week. Since I didn't have any friends who owned guns, I relied on teaching myself what I could through the web and from competition shooters I met on the range. I really enjoy learning new things, and there is an incredible amount of useful information online to help you have fun shooting.

Staying focused on having fun enabled me to stay calm under pressure, and that calmness helped me beat out seventeen *Top Shot* competitors. Many of my competitors psyched and stressed themselves out, since the competition wasn't a fun game for them as much as it was a title to be won or lost.

For me, competing was for fun and for the personal challenge—to see if I could come out on top. Having fun, constantly challenging myself, and striving to be my best is an attitude I carry with me in all the things I do in life. If I'm not enjoying or challenging myself, whether at work or play, then I'll seek a different path.

For Self-Defense

If your interest in shooting lies in learning how to defend yourself against attack, then I would suggest taking lessons specifically geared toward using firearms defensively. My book will help you with firearms basics, but self-defense training is a whole additional level of technical and physical skill that also carries ethical and legal considerations.

The United States has varying laws and regulations regarding how, when, and where you can use a firearm in self-defense. It depends on whether you are on your own property as well as the particular situation. In many counties, to carry a concealed firearm you must receive a permit from local law enforcement. However, certain counties do not require a permit, and there are additional laws regarding long guns (rifles and shotguns). Again, using a firearm for self-defense requires further study outside the confines of this book.

I'll go into a little bit more detail on this topic in part II on pistols in this book.

Increasing Physical Awareness

If you've never shot a gun before, you've probably seen guns on TV or in the movies. You might have seen some actor running at full speed, jumping away from an explosion while shooting a pistol in the air at some bad guy 40 yards away, and actually hitting his target. Let me tell you that even standing still, with no explosions and no distractions, some pistol shots you see on TV and in the moves are incredibly unrealistic.

When shooting, you will become hyperaware of how even the slightest movement—a leg twitch, a quick finger, the wind, and even your own breathing—can throw off a shot. Shooting is an activity that requires full body awareness, where becoming aware of and controlling your gross and fine motor skills are big keys to success.

Handling Stress

I know how my body reacts when I am stressed out. I feel my blood pressure rise and my face starting to feel warm. I can feel my heartbeat through my neck. My hunger usually goes away, and I actually feel quite alive, lucid, and in the moment. My senses are heightened, and I tend to perform well under stress.

At Google, I was surrounded by high performers who want to change the world. It is a "work hard, play hard" environment. I started my Google career as a technical support agent for Google Apps, which is basically a paid version of Gmail, Google Calendar, Google Docs, and other communication and productivity applications. My job was working directly with customers via email, phone, and chat to help them resolve any problems they were experiencing with the product.

As you can imagine, nobody is happy contacting tech support. Customers are already stressed out because there's a problem that's disrupted their life in some way. In my customer interactions, often the customer had a problem with email (and most of the time the problem was user error). In my five years at Google, I had spoken to thousands of customers, a number of whom were very upset. I learned how to handle that type of stress at work, and I've taken that same approach to handling stress into other situations, personal and professional.

Specifically, I tend to destress when I'm able to talk something through with a trusted individual. Taking a brisk walk and going outside also help. Breathing is really important, and so I become highly conscious of my breaths. Oftentimes I will exaggerate my inhalations and exhalations as a way of ensuring good oxygen flow. If you watch episodes of *Top Shot* Season 4, you will see me taking plenty of breaths during the competitions.

Body awareness is a skill that you can develop and apply to many parts of your life.

One of the most important techniques we'll discuss in this book is trigger squeeze. Having a strong sense of body awareness and control is a key concept you'll need to develop as a marksman. As it applies to physical awareness, trigger squeeze is all about focusing on one tiny part of your trigger finger, making sure it is properly pulling the trigger.

Increasing your physical awareness can also translate into other parts of your life. Perhaps you will become more aware of how your body reacts when stressed at work and how you go about calming yourself down. That approach could then be applied in a self-defense situation where you are under stress, or perhaps at the range when you are trying to steady yourself for a precision shot.

Increasing Your Mental Toughness

Marksmanship involves mental discipline as well as physical skill one. You should ask yourself how mentally disciplined you are. Do you have the mental stamina to dry-fire for five minutes and make sure you have perfect form each time? When you fall short, are you going to crumble or are you going to double down and practice even harder and smarter?

There will be certain aspects of marksmanship that will be hard. You may not be able to consistently hit the bull's-eye, and to figure out what's wrong when you don't. You may know what you have to do, but learning that habit may be challenging. Take comfort, though, in knowing that every shooter, no matter how experienced—including me—struggles with something.

The question is whether you have what it takes to overcome that hurdle. This book will teach you much about form and technique, but you will have to be mentally tough to push through some frustrating moments in which you will need to work on hard and practice. I promise you that, if you stick with it and practice, you will improve.

Exercising and Appreciating Your Second Amendment Rights

For American marksmen and markswomen, there can be no better way to appreciate a constitutional right than to exercise it. The Second Amendment protects our right to protect ourselves and our loved ones. If you are interested in Second Amendment politics, there is no shortage of interesting issues and debates in which you can engage.

If you live outside the United States, I hope you have an opportunity to learn about marksmanship in your home country or when traveling abroad. For some foreigners, the Second Amendment is such a big draw they are willing to give up their citizenship of birth to become an American citizen.

Iain Harrison is one such person. Iain is the *Top Shot* Season 1 champion, editor of *RECOIL Magazine*, and author of the afterword in this book. After his native England banned civilian ownership of pistol ownership in 1997, Iain left his home country and came to the United States to become a US citizen. Harrison notes that the government "gave everyone the chance to hand in [their guns], or face ten years in prison. I decided at that point that I wanted to continue owning firearms, so I moved to the United States."

Participating in the self-defense, competition, or fun use of firearms is one of the best ways to exercise and appreciate our Second Amendment rights.

Leadership

In the shooting community, there are plenty of opportunities for leadership. Many gun clubs and organizations need officers for a range duties, from administration, to finances, recruitment, community relations, fundraising, and social and competition activities.

In the policy and political realms, there are many opportunities to get involved at the local, state, and national levels.

Collecting

Much of the world's history can be told through firearms. Collecting firearms, whether family heirlooms or guns with historical significance, can hold special meaning to the owner. There is a large collectors market where gun owners trade, sell, and barter all sorts of interesting and historical firearms.

A Nazi Luger Pistol

For me, reading about history can sometimes be bland, and also hard to grasp unless I have an experience to anchor it. Visiting a historical site, touching a historical object, or hearing a first-hand story helps me remember the details.

With my *Top Shot* prize winnings, I wanted to invest in a historical firearm, one that had an interesting story.

The author's personal Luger pistol.

I found a Luger pistol that had weaved its way through Europe from World War I to World War II and eventually found its way to me here in the United States.

The pistol started out as a 1917 Artillery Luger and, after World War I, was issued a 4-inch new barrel and stamped "1920" to be issued to the new German army, which could not exceed 100,000 men, according to the Treaty of Versailles. My Luger was again reissued in 1937 with Nazi proof marks, a holster, and magazines. It was used from then until 1945, when an American soldier liberated it from a German soldier. When I purchased the gun, included were a German soldier's Iron Cross, Second Class with a ribbon, and a map of France written in German. On the back of the map is a calendar with written dates through March 11, 1945. That was the date the pistol was relieved from its owner.

The soldier passed this Luger to his daughter, who ended up selling it through an auction house. That's where I came upon it and appreciated its history and place in the world. It is one of my favorite firearms, and, at the time of this writing, I have only shot a few rounds through it and was impressed at how accurate it is almost seventy years later.

Many firearms increase in value over time, and, besides having monetary value, historic firearms are incredible pieces of our human history. Every time I pick up my Luger, I think about its path and the people who built the parts, the soldiers who relied on it, the lives saved and lost, and how it was a part of two world wars. Collecting firearms is a wonderful way to remember, respect, and preserve our history.

Hunting

At its core, hunting is about providing food for one's self and loved ones. Hunting is also about respecting and conserving our natural open space, and about controlling animal populations. Each season "tags" are distributed by each state's department tasked with regulating hunting and fishing. The number of tags for any given season is determined by state wildlife specialists to keep a balance in the ecosystem.

In a world so dominated by computers, phones, and video games, enjoying the great outdoors as a hunter is something I've just recently had the opportunity to experience. While many hunters hunt out of necessity to feed their families and protect their land and crops from varmints, there is also a huge social component to being outside and using all your senses. You get to spend some real quality time with friends and loved ones, uninterrupted time where you get to live in the moment instead of through an electronic screen.

My First Turkey Hunt

Many Americans associate turkeys with Thanksgiving and sandwich meat. You see turkey in plastic wrap at the supermarket and have probably seen some pictures and video of real turkeys.

I was invited on a shotgun turkey hunt with some NRA instructors the week I got my NRA instructor certification. We were at Red Bank Outfitters, a beautiful private ranch in Northern California learning about specific animal habits and characteristics. I learned how turkeys can see well, which is why hunters need to dress in camouflage from head to toe. If a turkey spots you, they will run, and hours of sitting patiently waiting can be all for naught with one wrong move.

I also learned about box and slate calls, and how to produce different calls with each. It was a thrill to be outdoors trying to see who would prevail in this game of man vs. turkey.

Unfortunately for us (but fortunately for the turkeys), the turkeys won. We spent ten hours over two days looking for gobblers, and we only found one that was on another property. We waited to see if any of the birds would cross the property line so we could at least take a shot, but to no avail.

Many hunts end without a single shot fired. That's the nature of the hunt. Sometimes it's good; other times you go home empty handed. But even if you don't bring any meat home, you still bring home memories of time with friends, of learning about the land, and of how to properly take from the land.

I'm excited for my next hunt and hope you will consider enjoying the great outdoors with me!

I also love food, and hunting for me has been a great way to reconnect with where food actually comes from. Having grown up in the suburbs, I ran the risk of learning that a chicken's natural state was growing in a Styrofoam tray. Thankfully, hunting has been an ethical, philosophical, and educational experience for me.

Survival Training

Perhaps you've been watching too much of *The Walking Dead* like I have, but knowing how to shoot a gun is a critical skill in the event you're stuck in some unsavory environment, for whatever reason. A more realistic scenario is if civil society ever breaks down and you're in a survival scenario.

When I was twelve years old, I was less than an hour away from the 1992 Rodney King riots where Korean American store owners had to rely on their own weapons to defend their lives and property because law enforcement and military personnel were unprepared, overwhelmed, and unable to provide security for everyone in South Central Los Angeles. Obviously, civil society breaking down is going to be a rare occurrence (at least I would like to think that in the United States), but it can, and has, happened.

Thinking back to when I was twelve years old watching events unfold on TV, all I understood at the time was that this was a race riot, and that guns were keeping people safe.

Now as an adult, I think about how, amongst other guns, I would at least want my AR-15 in that kind of lawless situation. (AR stands for ArmaLite, the company who originally designed the AR-15 platform. The AR-15 later became the M-16, used by militaries around the world.)

For Sport

Now here's an area that could change your life. For years and years, I went to a gun range and shot on a static firing line at paper targets.

After an hour of destroying a bunch of paper, I would get bored and pack it up. Then I discovered competition shooting.

Competition shooting has many different disciplines: United States Practical Shooting Association (USPSA), International Defensive Pistol Association (IDPA), skeet and trap shooting, rifle shooting, cowboy action, and 3-gun (pistol, rifle, shotgun). Among the many other competition shooting disciplines are ones specifically for youngsters, college students, and veterans.

Multi-time world champion Julie Golob inspires current and future shooters alike.

Many of these disciplines feature shooting from the holster and on the move at metal plates, paper targets, flying clays, wagons or other moving contraptions. One 3-gun competition, the MGM Ironman, even has a stage where you get hooked up to a zip line!

Anyone that is capable of completing a half-day safety training course can come compete. Amateurs and professionals alike come to matches all around the world. There are different classifications and divisions, so you are competing against shooters who are equally matched in both skill and gear. Most matches occur on the weekends, which is when most folks are available.

If you're interested in getting into competitive shooting, check out the end of parts II through IV of this book, on pistols, rifles, and shotguns, respectively.

For Community

Gun folk are some of the nicest people you will ever meet. Like any activity, there are social events and communities around varying demographics. There are many clubs for skeet and trap, competition, home defense and self-defense, clubs for young adults and women, and state organizations.

For those politically inclined, there are plenty of Second Amendment groups of like-minded Americans to join.

Competitions are primarily driven by volunteers who help create and build stages, keep score, serve as safety and range officers, fundraise, and recruit new shooters and sponsors. These volunteers are crucial in ensuring that the shooting community can operate smoothly.

What's great about shooting for me is that, after spending so much time behind a computer, my phone, and TV, I get to spend some time outdoors to relax, unplug, and socialize with fellow shooters.

Even if you aren't getting into shooting for the community aspect, I guarantee that, if you spend some time at a range or at events, you'll see how vibrant and diverse our community is.

Chapter Summary:

- Know your answer to the question "Why do you want to learn how to shoot?" It will be your guiding light throughout your journey into marksmanship.
- You may have many answers to the question above.
- The answers may possibly change over time, and that is OK. Adapt with your circumstances.

PART TWO: PISTOLS

CHAPTER FIVE

PISTOL BASICS

Let's get familiar with the mechanics and principles of a pistol. At a high level, a firearm has a tube, otherwise known as a barrel, made out of metal. Modern pistols are one type of firearm that fires a metallic cartridge. A cartridge contains a bullet and powder (we'll go into further detail in the next chapter). When the powder ignites, it propels a bullet out of the cartridge, through the barrel, toward the target.

At the rear end of the barrel—the end closest to the user when pointing the pistol—is the breech. The opposite end, where the bullet exits the barrel, is the muzzle. Pistols that fire metallic cartridges are breech-loading pistols. Back in the old days, pistols were called muzzleloaders because powder and a metal ball were loaded from the muzzle end. Muzzleloaders could generally only fire one shot per barrel and were slow to load.

Going Old School

On *Top Shot* Season 4, we competed with the Kentucky Flintlock pistol. It's a primitive muzzleloader that requires the shooter to manually load powder and the bullet into the muzzle, and then add a powder charge that is ignited by a piece of flint attached to the hammer. One thing unique about such a flintlock pistol is the delay of one to three seconds between pulling the trigger, the powder igniting, and the bullet exiting the muzzle. This can be an eternity if you're used to the faster ignition of a modern pistol and centerfire ammunition.

A Kentucky flintlock pistol—notable for its place in American colonial history, and for its use by seafaring pirates. Photo courtesy of HISTORY.

For me, good trigger control and not being surprised by the shot were critical components to learning how to shoot a Kentucky flintlock pistol. We'll be discussing trigger control later in this book. I only had about 8–10 minutes to handle and practice with the weapon, and so I heavily relied on the basic fundamentals of marksmanship to help me win with this pistol.

Both older and newer muzzleloader pistols are available, but since they are not as common as revolvers and semiautomatic (or "semiauto") pistols, they are not reviewed much in this book. There are other fantastic resources to learn more about muzzleloaders. They are a lot of fun to shoot, and I hope you get to shoot one someday.

A breech-loading pistol has three major components: the frame, the barrel, and the action.

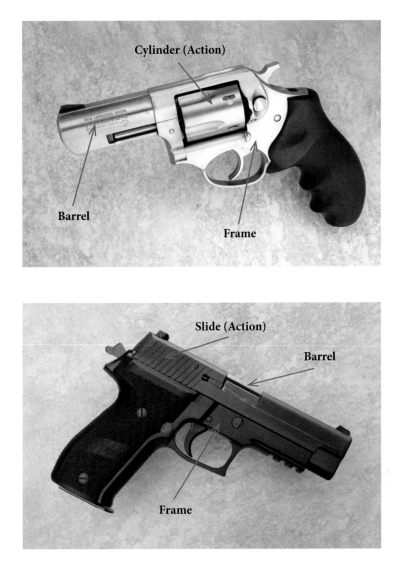

Frame

The frame is the piece that houses the action parts and, in a semiauto pistol, connects to the slide. The frame is the core pistol part to which everything else is attached. The grips are attached to the frame as well. Frames are typically made of metal or polymer. The trigger guard and rear sight (on revolvers) are also part of the frame. For semiautos, the rear and front sights are typically both on the slide. The front and back straps are in the designated spots between the grips.

Barrel

As previously noted, a barrel is a metal tube through which the bullet passes through. The barrel has a front sight on top. The section between the breech and the muzzle is the bore. Modern pistol barrels have bores that contain rifling, which is the set of spiral grooves you'll see when looking through a stand-alone barrel. (The only time it is OK to look down a barrel is if you have a firearm completely disassembled and the action is separated from the barrel.) The spiral grooves impart a spin on the bullet as it travels through the barrel, and this spin increases accuracy and keeps the bullet on target.

Pistol barrel lengths generally range from 3 to 7 inches. I would say that "standard" barrel length for a new shooter is in the 4- to 6-inch range. Generally speaking, shorter barrels equal more recoil. Of course, this also depends on what kind of caliber you end up choosing. Caliber is a measurement of the bore diameter in either inches or millimeters. We'll review these topics further in later sections.

At the breech end, the area where the cartridge is seated, is the chamber. "Chamber" can also be used as a verb, as in "chamber a round in the gun" which means to load a round into the chamber.

The slide is a part found only in semiautos. It is a metal piece that houses the barrel. The slide rides on rails on top of the frame, and slides to the rear and front with each shot.

Finally, some pistol barrels have threads at the muzzle end for suppressors. A suppressor (also known as a silencer or "can" in slang) is a fully enclosed piece of metal with baffles inside that redirects the hot gases in a way that not only reduces recoil and muzzle flash but also reduces the sound. Some people do not call it a "silencer" since it doesn't actually "silence" a gunshot but rather just drastically reduces the noise.

If you live in a certain state where suppressors are legal, then you're lucky. If your barrel does not have threads, you can either buy a threaded barrel to replace it, or you can send your barrel to a gunsmith, who can thread the barrel for you.

Action

The action is the combination of physical parts of the pistol that load, fire, and unload the gun. The trigger, hammer, cylinder, cylinder release, slide stop, takedown lever, magazine release, ejector rod, slide, and safety mechanisms are parts of the action.

While there are many pistol action types, we're only going to review the common ones here, namely single-action, double-action, and double-action.

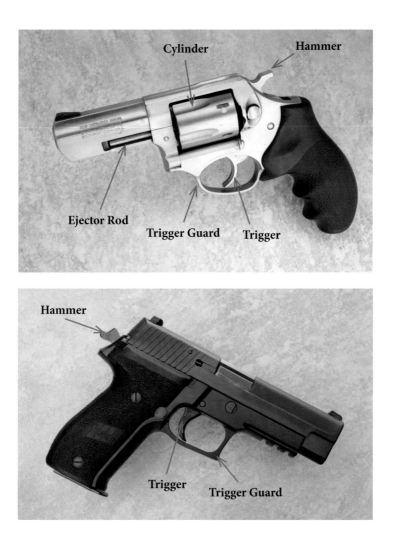

Single-Action (SA)

A gun is considered to be single-action if squeezing the trigger performs only one action—dropping the hammer to strike the cartridge. Single-action triggers usually require four to eight pounds of force. Competition guns can be made even lighter, requiring as little as two pounds of pressure to pull the trigger.

Double-Action (DA)

In double-action guns, squeezing the trigger performs two actions: cocking the hammer, and also dropping the hammer. To fire subsequent shots on a single-action revolver, the user must cock the hammer before each shot. Since the trigger is performing two jobs, it normally takes a lot more pressure to pull a double-action trigger. Between eight and fifteen pounds is common.

Double-Action/Single-Action (DA/SA)

In a DA/SA pistol, the first shot is double-action, but subsequent ones are single-action.

Law enforcement agencies often prefer DA/SA pistols, since the first trigger pull is a heavier double-action one that will reduce accidental discharges due to nerves, stress, or other factors officers experience out in the field. The lighter single-action trigger pull is then available on subsequent shots.

Double-Action Only (DAO)

DAO is just like double-action, except that every single trigger squeeze is double-action. This action type is targeted toward law enforcement personnel who want a heavier trigger pull on each shot to help prevent an accidental discharge. Even though DAO pistols are common amongst law enforcement, civilians are able to purchase DAO pistols.

Revolvers

A revolver differs from a semiautomatic pistol in that the revolver has a cylinder that revolves with each shot. The cylinder has anywhere from five to eight chambers, each of which can hold one cartridge each. Every time the hammer is cocked, the cylinder rotates and aligns a cartridge with the barrel.

A single-action revolver requires you to manually cock the hammer each time to fire a shot. A double-action revolver enables you to perform two actions with each trigger pull: cock and drop the hammer. If you have an exposed hammer (some revolvers have a concealed hammer), as you pull the trigger to the rear you will see it cock rearward. The trigger will reach a breaking point where the hammer will then drop as the user completes the trigger pull. Every revolver (and firearm for that matter) is unique; even the same make and model firearm may have slight variances in trigger pull. It's important to get acquainted with a firearm's trigger pull, which will enable you to improve your accuracy.

A double-action pistols with an exposed hammer usually can also be fired in single-action. If a double-action pistol does not have an exposed hammer, it can only be fired in double-action. Many pistols designed for personal protection are double-action only, since in a stressful situation you don't want to accidentally discharge a round; the heavier trigger pull helps prevent that from occurring.

Loading and Unloading a Revolver

Loading a revolver is pretty straightforward. There are two main options: through a loading gate or by swinging the cylinder away from the pistol. (*Note:* Most revolvers are for right-handed shooters. Left-handers using a right-handed revolver should follow the steps below. Use the opposite hands only when using a left-handed revolver, which is identified by the cylinder popping out to the right side of the frame.)

The Ruger Vaquero as featured on *Top Shot* Season 4's "The Perfect Run" episode. The loading gate is denoted by a red box. Photo courtesy of HISTORY.

The loading gate is a small piece of metal that flips away from the revolver and exposes one chamber in the cylinder. You must load one round at a time, rotating the cylinder by hand each time. Once the loading gate is closed, you should spin the cylinder back and forth until it locks in place. This means that a chamber and cartridge are aligned with the hammer and barrel and is now ready to fire.

Once you are ready to unload, make sure the hammer is down, unless your revolver requires a "half-cock," which is where the hammer must be cocked half way back to unlock the cylinder. Also make sure your finger is off the trigger throughout the unloading process. When you flip the loading gate back up, there will be an ejector rod to push each individual cartridge out. You must push and release the ejector rod to eject each cartridge, and then rotate the cylinder and repeat until empty. If you do not fire all the cartridges, they can also be ejected along with the empties.

The second load and unload option is by swinging the cylinder away from the pistol. If your revolver has this feature, there will be a cylinder release latch on the left side of the pistol, behind the cylinder.

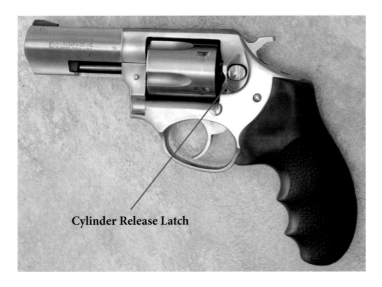

Cylinder Release Latch

To load, hold the revolver with your left hand, making sure to keep your finger off the trigger and your hand away from the muzzle. With your right hand, press the release latch, and use the pointer and middle fingers on your left hand to push the cylinder to the left of the pistol. You can now load cartridges into each chamber of the cylinder. Once complete, roll the cylinder back into the frame until you hear and feel a click that denotes the cylinder is locked. Spin the cylinder in both directions until you feel the cylinder lock.

A special note here about closing the cylinder: I'm sure you have seen people on TV and the movies use a wrist flip to close the cylinder. While it may look cool, it can screw up your revolver, so you should never close a cylinder in this fashion. The alignment of the cylinder with the barrel, as well as the timing of the cylinder rotating in conjunction with the trigger pull, can be affected. Flipping the cylinder can cause jams, misfires—and worse, an explosion of flying metal in your hand—if part of the bullet shears off the barrel as it leaves the chamber. The proper way to close the cylinder is to use your support hand to push the cylinder closed.

To unload, keep your finger off the trigger while pointing the gun up in a safe direction. Repeat the same steps to release the cylinder.

To eject the shells, push the ejector rod; the empty cartridges generally will drop out. Sometimes you may have to manually pull cartridges out, but the ejector rod will at least make the task easier.

There's also a top break-action type of revolver where the loading and unloading processes are similar to the swing-out cylinder method. To find out the appropriate loading and unloading method for your specific revolver, please consult your owner's manual or a knowledge-able party.

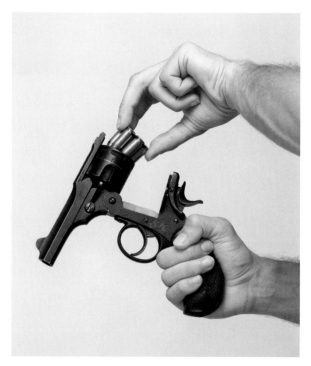

A break-action revolver.

Decocking

At times, you may be in the middle of firing your revolver and need to lower a cocked hammer. One example is if you are at a firing range and you hear a "cease fire" command. Once that command has been issued, you cannot fire your revolver to drop the hammer—you must lower it, or decock it manually.

To decock a revolver, make sure your trigger finger is off the trigger. Then place your support-hand thumb (left thumb if you are right-handed) in between the cocked hammer and the frame. This is a safety precaution in the event you lose control of the hammer, in which case your thumb will stop the hammer. Place your right thumb on the hammer, making sure you have a firm grip on the hammer. Pull the trigger while holding the hammer back until you feel the hammer release forward. Remove your support-hand thumb from the front of the hammer, and use your right thumb to slowly guide the hammer forward and down.

Safety Mechanisms

Revolvers generally do not have active safeties such as those on semiautomatic pistols. The assumption is that a heavier, double-action trigger pull and the need to manually cock the hammer will reduce the likelihood of an accidental discharge. As usual, make sure you are following the Four Rules of Firearm Safety as noted in chapter 2.

Revolver Grip

The shooting hand goes around the grip of the frame, and the support hand comes in on top of your shooting had. The thumb on your support hand should be on top of the thumb of your shooting hand. The reason for this is so you can cock the hammer with your support thumb without breaking your grip.

One-hand and two-hand revolver grips.

You should be gripping the pistol tightly enough to keep the pistol in your hands with each shot, but not so tight that your knuckles turn white. Exerting too much energy on the grip can throw your shot off, since your muscles will get tired faster. However, this really depends on the particular person. My recommendation is to start by gripping tightly to get a sense for that particular revolver's recoil with the particular ammo you're using. Then you can back off on the pressure until you find a good balance, where your hand and forearm muscles are in control and relaxed.

Semiautomatic Pistols

While revolvers and semiauto pistols have many of the same parts, there are some stark contrasts. A defining characteristic of a semiautomatic pistol is its use of a magazine to hold cartridges, in contrast to the cylinder on a revolver. Another semiauto characteristic is that one shot is fired with each trigger pull, and the action ejects and loads each round from a magazine. Specifically, the force from a fired round pushes the slide back, which ejects the spent cartridge out the ejection port. This slide movement also cocks the hammer, striker, or firing pin. As the slide returns forward through spring-loaded tension, it catches the top cartridge in the magazine and loads it into the chamber.

Magazines

Magazines have the following parts:

Body
The outer part of the magazine, which is made of metal or plastic in a rectangular box shape.

Follower and Spring
The "follower and spring" is a spring-loaded metal or plastic piece that pushes cartridges in an upward direction.

Floorplate
The floorplate is a piece of metal or plastic that holds the follower and spring inside the body. It can be removed to clean all the magazine parts.

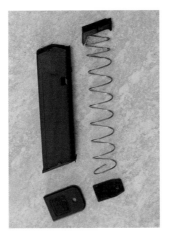

A disassembled Glock 17 magazine showing (clockwise from upper left) the body, the follower and spring, the magazine "insert" (not all magazines have this), and the floorplate.

Note that the proper nomenclature as it relates to semiautomatic pistols is just "magazine," not "clip" or "magazine clip." Clips are a different type of loading accessory. The defining characteristic is that clips do not have a spring loading mechanism. Moon clips allow for the fast reloading of revolvers, and on the rifle side the M1 Garand (infamous for its metal "ping" sound when the rifle is empty) uses clips.

Various types of moon clips.

An M1 Garand clip.

One advantage of semiautomatic pistol magazines is that they generally hold more cartridges than a revolver cylinder. Anywhere between eight and twenty-three rounds is standard for semiauto magazine capacity. Higher capacity magazines are available for many pistol models. Magazine capacity varies state to state, so make sure to check your local and state laws, or with your local gun store. Magazines enable faster reloads, which is another distinct advantage.

A drawback of semiautomatic pistols and their magazines is that they can sometimes contribute to jams and malfunctions. (See chapter 8 for descriptions on how to identify and clear jams). With more moving parts, a semiauto pistol can occasionally jam and not fire. Revolvers have fewer moving parts and have a reputation for being more reliable. However, semiauto pistols have become very reliable in modern times, so opinions continue to differ between the reliability of each platform.

Certain pistol magazines can accept baseplate extensions, which not only increases a magazine's capacity but provides a larger baseplate area to assist with loading.

Magazines from left to right: ten-round single-stack, seventeen-round double-stack, seventeen-round double-stack with a Taran Tactical baseplate extension, and a thirty-three-round double-stack.

Single-stack and double-stack: Some magazines are single-stack, which means that the cartridges are stacked one on top of the other inside the magazine. Double-stack is where the bullets are stacked side-by-side inside the magazine. A benefit of double-stack magazines is that they can hold more ammunition, but oftentimes this adds more width in both the magazine and pistol. More ammunition will also increase the overall weight of a loaded pistol.

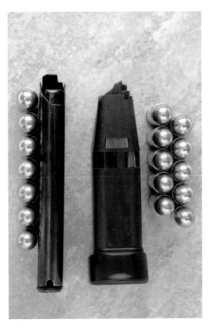

(Left to right) Single-stack and double-stack magazines showing how the rounds stack up.

With regards to reliability, both single- and double-stack magazines are generally reliable. Both types contain the same parts: body, follower and spring, and baseplate. One type does not jam more or less frequently, but this can vary with the combination of pistol, magazine size or brand, and the cleanliness of your magazine and pistol. Users should test different combinations to determine the optimal configuration.

Some semiautomatic pistols only accept either single- or double-stack magazines, while others can accept both. You can find out this information on the manufacturer's website, at a gun shop, or by searching the web for the types of magazines sold for a specific make and model.

Generally speaking, magazines are not interchangeable between different makes and models. For example, you cannot take any 9mm pistol magazine and use it in any pistol. Magazines are made for a specific make and model of pistol. Oftentimes the magazine will be stamped with the make and caliber. Sometimes the model may also be included. If you own multiple pistols, it can help to label each magazine to help you remember which magazines go to which pistol.

Sometimes different models of a manufacturer's pistol can use the same magazine. For example, the Glock 17 and 34 use the same magazines, either single- or double-stack.

Loading a Magazine

Loading a magazine, or mag, can be tricky when you're first learning this skill. With practice, you will build muscle strength in your fingers to do it quickly. With your weak hand (left hand if you're right-handed, and vice versa), hold the magazine with the front end pointing away from you. Take one round with the bullet end pointing away from you, and push it down on the front part of the follower, and then back to the rear wall of the magazine. You should now have one round in the magazine.

To continue loading, push down on the back half of the cartridge with your weak-hand thumb. With your strong hand, push a second round on top of the first one, making sure that the second round is forward enough to clear the magazine lips. Slide the second round to the rear wall just as you did with the first round. Continue until the magazine is filled to capacity. Many magazines have indicators that tell you how many rounds are currently loaded.

Alternatively, there are speed loaders available that will enable you to dedicate more energy to shooting rather than to loading.

A LULA® speed loader.

Once your magazine is loaded, it's generally a good idea to take the rear of the magazine and give it a solid tap in your hand or on a hard surface. This helps properly seat all of the cartridges to prevent jams and misfeeds.

New magazines can be particularly hard to load because the spring is new and hasn't been broken in. There are third-party speed loaders that you can use to load faster, which will also save your hand strength. Many competition shooters use speed loaders, since we want to save our strength and energy for the competition instead of wasting it on loading magazines.

I also recommend using a permanent marker to write your name on your magazines. (Take it from me, I accidentally left six Glock magazines at the range and only realized it a week later. The magazines had disappeared. I now have my name on all my mags). Numbering your magazines is also a good idea in the event that one of them malfunctions. You'll then be able to remember and identify the problem mag once you get home from the range.

Loading and Unloading

Loading a semiautomatic pistol takes some practice. Like anything else, start slowly and you'll get better as you get more experienced and confident. Before starting, remember to confirm that the gun is unloaded by performing a visual and manual chamber check: look and touch the chamber to confirm it is empty.

To start the loading process, place the pistol in your firing hand and the magazine in your support hand, with the cartridges facing in the same direction as the muzzle. Bring the magazine up into the magazine well, which is located on the bottom of the frame, under the grips. As you insert the magazine in an upward direction, bring the palm of your weak hand under the magazine and hit it two to three times to properly seat the magazine. If you do not do this, you run the risk of the magazine falling out.

To charge the pistol (i.e., to chamber a round), first make sure your finger is off the trigger. Then, grasp the rear part of the slide with your thumb and pointer (first) finger and pull the slide all the way back. Simply let go of the slide and the spring will pull it forward and chamber the top cartridge. This is colloquially known as "slingshotting"—and is the most simple technique. The pistol is now ready to fire.

When slingshotting, you want to make sure that you let go of the slide after pulling it back and avoid easing the slide forward. Called "riding the slide"—this can cause feeding jams, since a semiauto pistol is designed to leverage the spring-loaded force of the slide.

Alternatively, if the slide is already locked to the rear, it can be closed by pressing the slide-lock release.

Keeping your finger off the trigger during the load process is vital—an accidental discharge can occur by pulling the trigger as you rack the slide.

Slide Lock

A pistol slide will lock to the rear in one of two ways: 1) Shooting to slide lock: the slide locks when a pistol fires its last shot and there is an empty magazine in the pistol. You should always double-check to make sure it's not a malfunction. 2) The user manually locks the slide back.

To lock a slide if you're right-handed, you will keep your finger off the trigger and hold the pistol normally in your strong hand. However, you'll want to swing your thumb and hand clockwise around the grip so your thumb can reach the slide stop. With your strong-hand thumb, push the slide stop up—you may or may not feel it move at this point, but keep applying upward pressure. With your support hand, grip the slide over the top rear of it and push the slide to the rear. The slide should lock against the slide stop.

To manually lock a semiauto pistol slide back: 1) Grab the pistol with your shooting hand. With your support hand, grab the top rear of the slide.

2) While holding the slide in place, push the frame forward with your shooting hand.

3) With your shooting-hand thumb, lift up the slide stop (pictured above thumb). Note that you may need to rotate your shooting hand around the grip to get proper thumb placement.

4) Your pistol is now slide locked.

For left-handers, you can do it like right-handers, or you can take your support-hand thumb and lift the slide stop up while pulling the slide back with the same hand. There are a number of other alternative methods, so I advise consulting the web or a knowledge source.

There are a few pistol brands and models available for left-handed shooters, which is another great option.

To unload a semiautomatic pistol, start by placing your finger off the trigger and pointing the gun in a safe direction. Locate and depress the magazine release button with your thumb. On many pistols, it is on the left side of the frame. However, some pistols have an ambidextrous safety near the same location. Check your instruction manual for the exact location of your magazine release. You will likely need to rotate your shooting hand clockwise around the grip to reach the release, which is normal. If the magazine does not slide out on its own, pull it out with your weak hand.

One really important thing to note here is that, even though you have removed the magazine, it is possible for a live round to be in the chamber. You can still pull the trigger and fire a shot with the magazine out of the gun. This is why it is important to keep your finger off the trigger when unloading, and also to follow the golden rule for safety: Always keep the gun pointed in a safe direction.

After you have removed the magazine, rack the slide at least three times to clear the chamber. Finally, perform a visual and manual chamber check to confirm the gun is unloaded.

Safety Mechanisms and Decocking

Modern pistols have safety mechanisms, which are either active (where a shooter must physically toggle a switch on or off) or passive (where the safeties work by firearm design). An active safety toggle switch usually offers "safe" and "fire" modes. A passive safety example is Glock's Safe Action® system, which has three passive safeties. Two are internal safeties, and the third prevents the trigger from being depressed unless the trigger safety is also engaged. This helps prevent an accidental discharge if the pistol is dropped or falls to the ground.

Some double-action semiautomatic pistols have a decocker, which is another type of safety. A decocker decocks the hammer and puts the pistol in double-action. A user can manually decock a pistol, as described in the revolver section. Manual decocking can be dangerous if the user isn't properly trained in that particular technique. It also violates one of the safety rules, keeping your finger off the trigger until ready to fire. A decocker will help maintain firearm safety rules.

A decocker enables safer decocking, since it is intended to block the hammer or firing pin. But remember, safeties are mechanical and can always fail. The only way to stay safe is to follow the Four Rules of Firearm Safety in chapter 2.

It's important to read your gun's instruction manual to learn which safety mechanisms are on your gun.

Chapter Summary

- There are three major components of a pistol:
  - Frame: Core pistol part to which everything else is attached.
  - Barrel: Metal tube through which the bullet passes. The muzzle end is where the bullet exits. The breech end is where the cartridge is loaded.
  - Action: The parts of the pistol that load, fire, and unload the gun. The trigger, hammer, cylinder, cylinder release, slide stop, takedown lever, magazine release, ejector rod, slide, and safety mechanisms are all part of the action.
- Types of pistol actions are single-action (SA), double-action (DA), double-action/single-action (DA/SA), and double-action only (DAO).
- Revolvers have a cylinder that contains the live cartridges. Every time the hammer is cocked, the cylinder rotates and aligns a cartridge with the barrel.
- Semiautomatics use magazines to hold cartridges. One shot is fired with each trigger pull, and the action ejects and loads each round from a magazine.
- Know your pistol's safety mechanisms.

CHAPTER SIX

PISTOL AMMUNITION

When I started shooting, I didn't give much thought to the ammunition, or ammo, I used. I picked ammunition based on price and chose a slightly higher-priced brand, assuming that would get me decent-quality ammo. While price is a factor with ammunition, understanding how ammunition works and the variables that affect performance and reliability can help you make an informed decision.

There are four basic components to a cartridge:
1. bullet
2. case, shell, or cartridge
3. powder
4. primer

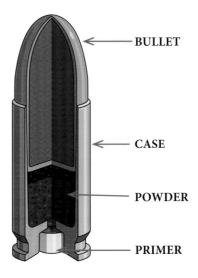

BULLET

CASE

POWDER

PRIMER

Bullet

Many people colloquially use "bullet" when they often mean cartridge, ammo, or round—all terms that denote a fully loaded cartridge. A bullet is the projectile that is loaded into a cartridge. A bullet by itself is just an inert hunk of metal. You can't "load a gun with bullets"; this would literally mean putting bullets somewhere into the gun, but it wouldn't be able to fire. A bullet must be combined with a case, powder, and primer to form a loaded cartridge, also called a round.

Bullets next to fully assembled cartridges.

There are many different shapes and forms of construction. "Ball" ammo is a standard type of bullet for target practice and other uses. Ball ammo is often a "full metal jacket" (FMJ), which means that the bullet is made of a lead core, and completely covered in a metal coating. This coating helps increase velocity, improve accuracy, and reduce the amount of metal deposits left in the barrel after each shot. Other types of bullets, such as hollow points, are meant to expand upon impact and have different designs and are made of different metals. This is only a small sampling of the many bullet shapes and materials available.

Case, Shell, or Cartridge

Most cases are made of brass, and you'll often hear shooters refer to cases as "brass." The case has an empty space for the powder and the primer. The case is marked with the specific caliber on the headstamp.

Headstamp on a .45ACP case.

Powder

Powder is the primary propellant in a cartridge.

Primer

I like to think of a primer as a snap cap. The hammer, striker, or firing pin of a pistol hits the primer, which creates a small spark. This in turn ignites the primary powder charge in the case, which in turn creates enough pressure to force the bullet out of the case.

Rimfire vs. Centerfire Ammo

There are two basic types of ammunition: rimfire and centerfire. A rimfire cartridge is one where the rim of the cartridge needs to be struck by the weapon's firing pin. That force ignites a percussion cap, which in turn ignites the powder behind the bullet.

A centerfire cartridge is simply one where the center of the cartridge (instead of the rim) has the primer, which when struck, ignites the powder charge.

Some basic differences between the two:

Rimfire:
- They are generally available in smaller calibers, such as .17 and .22.
- They are not reloadable.

Centerfire:
- They are generally available in larger calibers.
- Users can save and reload the cartridges.

Rimfire ammo is generally cheaper than centerfire ammo, but it really depends on the quality of the bullet, powder, and the brand's reputation.

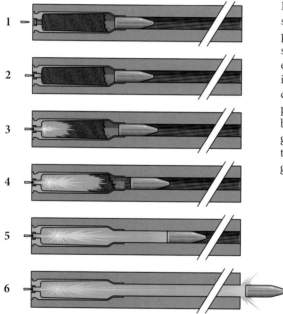

Pistol and rifle rounds have the same fire sequence: 1) Trigger pull releases firing pin, which strikes the primer; 2) primer explodes, creates a spark, and ignites the powder; 3) As powder burns, hot gas builds up pressure; 4) Hot gases force the bullet out of the case; 5) Hot gases propel the bullet through the barrel; 6) Bullet and hot gases exit the muzzle.

Caliber

Caliber is the diameter of a bullet at its widest point. Caliber is measured in both inches and millimeters. Sometimes the stated caliber includes the unit of measurement, such as "9mm," which would be spoken as simply "nine millimeter." Some caliber designations do not include the unit of measurement, such as ".40 caliber." The latter designations often include additional descriptors that signify a different case, or bullet length or shape, such as ".22LR," ".380ACP," ".38 Special." "ACP" stands for "Automatic Colt Pistol," which is different from .45 Long Colt and other types of .45 caliber cartridges.

There are too many calibers to list, but for the beginner I would advise focusing on the following (in ascending order of size): .22LR, .380ACP, .38 Special, 9mm, .40, and .45ACP. I recommend these calibers because they are widely available. You will want to research the cost of each to make sure you can afford to practice. The ammo will get more expensive as you go up in caliber, but certain types of match-grade and self-defense ammo can be more expensive because of special features and higher-quality components.

For your first gun, I recommend avoiding caliber designations with "magnum" in them, such as .357 and .44 magnum because such large-bore cartridges cause strong recoil in a firearm. Save that for your second, third, fourth guns and beyond, or find a friend or range to loan you one so you can try it out. Dirty Harry's Smith & Wesson Model 29 .44 Magnum is one pistol you have to shoot at some point in your life. Magnum rounds have increased powder loads, and while they are a ton of fun to shoot, they are not good to learn on because of the significant recoil. Unmanageable recoil can inhibit a beginner's development because learning the fundamentals of sight alignment and trigger control is that much harder.

Fun tip: If you ever want to start a vibrant discussion, ask a seasoned shooter what his or her preferred caliber is and why.

I highly recommend that beginner shooters buy factory-loaded ammo. As you progress in your training and interact with other shooters, you may discover reloaded ammunition that can be trusted.

One thing that almost all shooters recommend is saving your brass after firing a round.

On the left, a bullet in its case; on the right, the empty, fired brass.

This brass can be reused, which can save someone a lot of money. Even if you never plan on reloading your ammo yourself, you can sell your used brass to someone who wants to reload. It's basically free money lying on the ground at the range. One way of thinking about this is, why would you leave a bunch of nickels, dimes, and quarters just lying around?

A note on proper range etiquette: you should only collect your own brass in case other shooters want to keep their own. You're welcome to ask a fellow shooter if they plan to keep their brass. If they say no, you're welcome to grab it. Some ranges do not allow shooters to collect their own brass, which means the range is making money off of your empties. If you want to save your brass, the only option is to find a range or location that will allow you to collect your brass.

Chapter Summary:

- Bullet: A metal projectile that is seated in a cartridge.
- Case: Also known as a cartridge or a round, this holds the primer, powder, and bullet. There are two types: rimfire and centerfire. The former has the primer in the rim of the case, and the latter has the primer in the center of the headstamp. Centerfire cases are reloadable.
- Primer: The part of the cartridge that, when struck by the firing pin or hammer, ignites the primary powder charge.
- Powder: When ignited by the primer, powder creates the energy and pressure needed to expel the bullet out of the cartridge.
- Caliber: Measurement of the bullet's diameter at its widest point. Caliber measurements can be in inches of millimeters. Excellent beginner calibers are .22LR or 9mm.
- Factory Ammo: Ammunition that is made in a factory.
- Handloaded/Reloaded ammo: Ammunition that is made by hand, either from new components (such as brass, primer, and bullet) or lightly used brass that has been fired once or twice.

CHAPTER SEVEN

PISTOL MARKSMANSHIP FUNDAMENTALS

As a beginner, learning the fundamentals is critical to your future success. These include hand and eye dominance, which plays a significant role in pistol marksmanship. Hand dominance is straightforward. You're most likely right-handed or left-handed, but not ambidextrous. If you're right-handed, then your right hand is your "strong" or "shooting" hand and your left hand is your "weak" or "support" hand, vice versa for left-handers.

Eye dominance may be a new concept for you. Everyone has one eye that is more dominant than the other. You probably never notice this because, with both eyes open, the world just looks in focus and in proper perspective. Eye dominance can affect your accuracy so it's important to know your which of your eyes is dominant.

Determining Your Dominant Eye

Extend your arms and form a small triangle with your hands. Your fingers should almost completely overlap. Now look at an object 5 to 10 feet away through the triangle. Slowly bring your hands closer to the center of your face while keeping that object in sight.

Note that the arms are extended and the triangle size is small. Focus on an object about 10 feet away from you.

While keeping your focus on the object, bring your hands in until they are almost touching your face. Close your left eye. Do you see the object? That means your right eye is dominant. If you close your right eye and can see the object, then your left eye is dominant.

There are many shooters who are cross-dominant, which means their dominant eye is on their support side. Basically, a cross-dominant, right-handed shooter is left-eye dominant, and vice versa.

A number of different techniques are available to the cross-dominant shooter. To simplify things for the beginning shooter, I recommend using your dominant eye instead of trying to train your nondominant eye. For a right-handed, cross-dominant shooter, this means that you will keep your right eye closed and slightly shift the pistol to the left until you can get your sight picture and sight alignment.

If you are cross-dominant, I highly recommend searching online for additional techniques and philosophies.

One Eye or Two?

There are some different schools of thought as to whether shooting a pistol with one eye open or two is better. One eye tends to increase accuracy, but two eyes is often recommended in self-defense situations since, you then have your full peripheral vision to detect multiple threats. In pistol competition I shoot with both eyes open, but if I'm just going for accuracy and drilling rounds on top of one another, I opt for having only one eye open.

For beginner shooters, I recommend learning shooting with one eye open, since I believe it will help with your accuracy. With one eye open, you will not have as many distractions in your field of view, and that will enable you to focus on your target better. Once you are comfortable, feel free to explore shooting with two eyes open.

Now that we've determined your hand and eye dominance, let's dive into marksmanship fundamentals. There are five common denominators in pistol marksmanship, and they are the same for rifle marksmanship: aiming, breathing control, hold control, trigger control, and follow-through.

Aiming

Aiming is simply the process of aligning the pistol at the intended target so the bullet will hit the intended mark. You will need to use the pistol's sights to accomplish this. Firearms typically have a rear leaf or notch sight, and a front post. Aiming has two components: sight alignment and sight picture. Both are crucial in being accurate.

Sight alignment is all about aligning the two sights with your eye. The basic concept is that the top of the front sight post should be level with the top of the posts on the rear sight, and "daylight" (space) to the left and right of the front sight post should be equal.

Sight picture is aligning the sights to the target you are aiming at. Aligned sights won't do you any good if you aren't pointing them at the target. If you do not have a good sight picture (for example, something is obstructing your view, it is too bright or too dark, or there's a problem with your protective eyewear), then do not take the shot. Make sure your finger is off the trigger before you place your weapon down.

Every pistol shoots a little differently, and the sight picture may vary, too. To hit dead on, sometimes the aligned sights need to be placed directly on top of the target, other times you'll need to use a "six o'clock" hold. You'll hear the "o'clock" reference used a lot in shooting—simply imagine the face of a clock and the hours. A twelve-o'clock hold or position is the straight up direction, three o'clock is to the right, six o'clock is straight down, and nine o'clock is to the left.

If you are using iron sights, it is critical that you focus on your front sight when you are acquiring your sight picture. This means that your target and your rear sights will be blurry. The idea here is that your front sight post is the last point of exit for the bullet, and so keeping that front post steady and pointed on target is critical if you want to hit what you're aiming at.

Many shooters have their focus on the target (left) or their focus on the rear sight (right). When breaking a shot, the correct focus should be on the front sight (center).

Most new shooters' natural tendency is to focus on their target, but the problem is you're not paying as much attention to your sights to make sure your gun is pointing exactly where you want it to shoot. The front sight is above the muzzle, where the bullet exists, and so wherever the front sight is pointing is where the bullet is most likely to go. Trigger control and other factors also come into play, but remember that focusing on your front sight is the correct pistol sight picture.

Breathing Control

Holding a pistol and trying to keep the sights aligned and on target is difficult on its own. When your body's natural tendency to move when breathing is added in, hitting your target becomes even more difficult.

As you exhale you, should be taking the slack out of the trigger. When you have about one-third of your air left, pause. This is when you should take the shot. Your body is steady during this pause, which will help you with your sight alignment. You should take no more than five seconds to take the shot. If you need more time, take another breath and reset. Depriving your brain and body of oxygen will only make things more challenging.

Conversely, do not hold your breathe. *Top Shot* Season 1 competitor Kelly Bachand taught me that one of the first things to go when we are deprived of oxygen is our eyesight. So make sure to breathe when you shoot!

Hold Control

This is simply your body being able to hold the pistol steady while lining up your sights, getting a good sight picture, getting your breathe under control, and squeezing the trigger to take the shot. If you have not yet been able to practice enough to develop the right muscles to hold a pistol steady for a long time, feel free after each shot to take your finger off the trigger, lower your arm, and relax for a few seconds to reset. I've seen many new shooters rip off ten to seventeen shots without relaxing once. The hands, arms, and shoulders will start to shake. I encourage you to watch a new shooter do some slow accuracy shooting without taking a break to see this in effect. Even the pros know to rest every so often, because fatigue is going to set in and affect accuracy.

Trigger Control

Almost 100 percent of all new shooters instinctively pull a trigger incorrectly. Their finger usually looks like a piece of heavy flesh slamming back on the trigger, and then, as if their finger is made of bouncy rubber, it comes flying off the trigger. I can provide this vivid description because I remember how I was when I first started learning the proper technique.

The trigger's smooth movement backward, as well as forward, will greatly affect your accuracy and is something every marksman works to improve. Spastic, herky-jerky movements will negatively affect your accuracy. To demonstrate this point, dry-fire a pistol by pulling the trigger as quickly as you can, and rip your finger off the trigger. While doing this, focus on the front sight of the pistol and see how it moves around.

Here's the breakdown of proper trigger control:
1. Place the center of your trigger finger's first pad on the trigger.

2. Slowly take out the slack through a slow squeeze, and make sure you feel equal pressure on your trigger-finger pad. You need to squeeze *straight back*. Any left or right pressure will throw off your shot.
3. Feel for the trigger's breaking point.
4. Trap the trigger and follow through.
5. Reset.
6. Repeat.

After you take the shot, keep your front sight on target and pause for a beat or two. The idea here is that you do not want to lower the gun quickly, or raise your head, to look at your target. I've seen new shooters do exactly this while they are firing; consequently, either the barrel drops or the sight alignment gets thrown off, or both. Lowering the gun and raising your head are terrible habits you do not want to learn. Following through by keeping the gun up and on target for a beat or two after a shot is a simple technique to improve your accuracy.

If you're taking an immediate follow-up shot, release the pressure on the trigger slowly until you feel the reset "click." (I'm referring to a loaded, semiautomatic pistol. If you are practicing with an unloaded semiauto pistol, you will need to rack the slide before you release the pressure to feel the reset.) Then repeat steps 2 and 3 as needed.

Simplified, try to remember *press, trap, reset.*

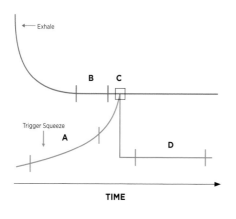

Bring your breathing and trigger squeezing together. A) Apply smooth pressure to the trigger. B) Near the end of your breath, keep your body still. C) Break the shot, trigger pressure drops, and trap the trigger. D) Follow through: Keep trigger trapped for 1–2 seconds. Slowly let off until you hear/feel the reset "click" and repeat firing sequence.

This sequence optimizes your movement efficiency by minimizing extraneous movement that could affect your accuracy and ability to send follow-up shots.

Baseball Camp: A Training Framework

I played a lot of Little League baseball as a kid, and four of my summers were spent at the Mark Cresse School of Baseball in Southern California. Mark Cresse was a Los Angeles Dodgers bullpen coach, and it was at his camp that I learned how to break down the mechanics of swinging a bat and throwing a ball, along with other skills, such as teamwork, communication, and good sportsmanship.

I specifically remember the five stages of batting and the hours and hours of drills we would go through. We would start by memorizing each stage with bat in hand. There would be no live batting until later, similar to dry-fire practice in the marksmanship world. Our coach would yell "Position 1! Position 2! And so forth." Our group of twelve-year-olds would follow his commands in unified choreography.

Learning or creating a framework you can rely on is critically important, regardless of whether you are trying to solve a physical activity or a complex business problem.

To highlight this, I will recap a *Top Shot* elimination challenge I competed in with a weapon called an "atlatl."

The loading and shooting sequence for an atlatl. Notice the follow-through in the final picture. You want a similar type of follow-through with your pistol and rifle trigger control.

An atlatl is a prehistoric spear-throwing weapon that I had never seen, nor heard of, before. I had one hour of one-to-one practice with an expert, Jack Dagger (gotta love the name), and during the training I created a "mental checklist" or framework around how to quickly learn this unfamiliar weapon. I used my past experience playing baseball (and golf) to create structure around using an atlatl in an internationally televised marksmanship competition. At the end of the day, marksmanship is about hitting something with a projectile, and so whether you learn marksmanship with a firearm, a rock, or a baseball, common marksmanship fundamentals—such as aiming, technique, focus, and form—all apply.

Some people ask me how I was able to compete under those stressful conditions, knowing that I could have been eliminated using a weapon I had never seen before. The confidence in my atlatl framework was the tool I needed to win.

Trigger-Finger Placement

For semiautomatic pistols, you want to place the trigger on the soft pad between the end of your trigger finger and the first joint.

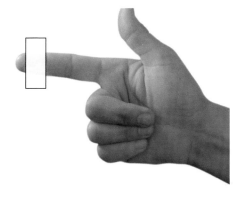

Align trigger with this part of your finger.

Some instructors may tell you that, if you're shooting a double-action revolver, using the crook of your first joint is fine, and I see nothing wrong with that approach if it works for you.

The goal here is to apply flat, even pressure towards you. A right-handed shooter who jerks the trigger is applying too much pressure on the left side, causing the shot to drop low and oftentimes to the left; vice versa for a left-hander. A great way to address this is to dry-fire. Marksmen at every level often practice a trigger squeeze with an empty gun and no ammunition in sight. You will know your trigger squeeze is getting good when you see your front sight post remain still after taking the shot. The goal is to consistently repeat this motion so it gets built into your muscle memory.

300–500 Repetitions

Some studies have shown that, for the average person, ingraining a fine motor skill can take 300–500 repetitions. Marksmanship is about putting in the time to practice refining each movement. You don't stop until it's as close to perfect as you can get it in that session. And then you keep working at it in later sessions. From your trigger squeeze to sight alignment, to other techniques, repetition is the only way to get as close to perfection as you can.

Another interesting finding is that relearning an old skill can take you anywhere from three to 5,000 repetitions to get back to your previous proficiency. I treat marksmanship like any other skill I want to either build or maintain: use it, or lose it!

One thing to note about trigger-finger placement is finding the right-size gun for your particular hands. If you have small hands and are handling a full-size pistol, you may not even be able to get your trigger finger on the trigger. You'll want to try shooting many different pistol models until you find one that enables you to apply all the basic fundamentals of marksmanship.

Surprise!

A shooter's first shot is oftentimes the best shot of that practice session. It is because the shooter is not anticipating any recoil, and simply lets the shot "surprise" them. Once you've fired a few rounds, you will most likely subconsciously drop the muzzle of the pistol in anticipation of the recoil, and you will see your shots drop below your point of aim. This is often called "flinching," where you're anticipating all the recoil, muzzle flash, and noise.

For the beginner, I recommend focusing on two pistol-shooting positions: benchrest and standing.

Benchrest

With the benchrest position, you will be able to minimize body-movement distractions and focus on the fundamentals (aiming, breathing control, trigger control, hold control, and follow-through). The benchrest position is pretty straightforward, but there are some points to remember:

1. Find a solid chair or bench where, ideally, your legs can rest naturally at a 90-degree angle with your feet planted flat on the floor.
2. Sit down and face the target.
3. Find a table or other solid surface where you can place a bag or other support. You want to have a support that is high enough so that when your arms rest on it, you can easily see the pistol sights without having to lean forward and scrunch your head down.

Notice how the bag is high enough so the shooter can easily see the pistol sights without having to strain his back.

Your shooting position forms the foundation of your shooting platform. An uncomfortable or unstable position can affect your accuracy, so it's important to learn and practice comfortable positions.

Standing

With standing positions, for beginners there are two basic options: isosceles and Weaver.

Isosceles Stance

If you don't remember geometry, an isosceles triangle has two equal sides. From a bird's eye view, the two equal sides are your arms, and your legs form the third side.

Your feet should be planted flat on the ground, a little wider than shoulder width apart. Knees should be slightly bent, and your upper body should be leaning slightly forward at the hips. While holding the pistol, your arms should be fully locked and pushed out toward your target.

A proper isosceles stance. Feet are a bit wider than shoulder length, and weight is equally balanced. Arms are locked.

Profile view: The shooter is bent a little forward at the hips, with knees slightly bent.

Improper isosceles stance. Knees are locked. Upper body is leaning back. Too much elbow bend. The shooter's stability is greatly reduced by each of these errors.

New shooters often arch their backs away from the pistol because they are afraid of the noise, recoil, and everything else. As the pictures above illustrate, the correct stance will provide you with much more stability and control. When you are stable and in control, you'll shoot better, with more confidence and accuracy.

Weaver Stance

Named after John Weaver (a Californian competition shooter in the 1950s) who developed the stance, the Weaver stance is popular in movies and TV. In the real world, it is used by law enforcement, military, and self-defense instructors. One of the primary benefits of the Weaver stance is that since your body is at an angle you are reducing your profile, and therefore decreasing the chances you will be hit if being shot at.

The Weaver stance. The feet are at a 45-degree angle, with the support foot forward. The shooting arm is locked or almost locked out. The support arm is slightly bent.

A proper Weaver stance starts with feet shoulder-width apart. Your shooting-side foot moves back about 8–10 inches so it forms an approximately 45-degree angle with your support foot. Your support foot should point towards the target, and your shooting foot should point about 45 degrees away from your body.

There are many variations on these two stances, but beginners can start with these two and build on this foundation.

Grip

A solid grip is crucial to creating a stable shooting platform. Remember, you are holding a weapon that contains an explosive charge that will transfer energy in many directions, notably back at you (and if the gun is misaligned with your body, possibly left or right), and straight up. The more stable you are, the better you can control the weapon and hit the intended target.

Let's start with the shooting hand, and specifically for semiautos. The first thing is establishing a high grip. The idea is that we want to get on top of the gun as much as possible to help counteract that recoil. Conversely, if we hold the gun way low on the grip, it would flip out of our hands.

A low grip does not provide a stable shooting platform. This particular pistol is also a little too big for this shooter's hands.

The thumbs can be forward, or they can be up.

On 1911-style pistols, Glocks, and other pistols that have a dovetail or similar anatomy above the backstrap, you want to eliminate any space you see between the webbing of your thumb and pointer finger.

A proper high grip with the shooting hand

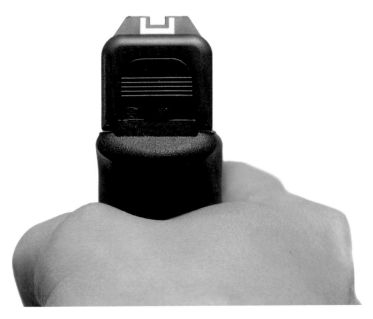

An improper low grip. Notice the large gap between the web of the hand and the top part of the grip.

The thumbs *should not* be placed on the back of the slide. The
slide cycles back with each shot, so your thumbs could be injured if they are behind the slide when shooting. Also notice the
poor low grip, where the shooting hand is too low.

Guide the heel of your support hand into the natural gap left by your
shooting hand.

Support hand approaching the grip.

Support hand locked in.

Say No to Tea Cups!

You may have seen some shooters put their support hand underneath the magazine well to create a "teacup." Not only is this a weak grip, it may lead to your chastisement at your local range. It is an outdated approach that I do not recommend.

Say "no" to tea cups!

A two-handed revolver grip is similar, but different in a few ways. The main difference is the location of your thumbs. You do not want to have your thumbs high or they may get burned by hot gases exiting the cylinder. For right-handers, keep your right thumb down and away from the cylinder, and your left thumb on top of the right. You can use your left thumb to cock the hammer with each shot, which enables you to maintain your grip between shots.

Isometric Tension

Let's talk about the concept of isometric tension. This is when two forces are pushing and pulling against each other but causing no movement. With respect to marksmanship, your hands are the forces, and you want to keep the pistol steady for sight-picture and alignment purposes. Isometric tension keeps the gun from moving in our hands and enables you to send faster follow-up shots.

Isometric tension is basically you pushing the gun forward with your shooting hand and pulling back with your support hand. Then, your support hand should provide about 70 percent of the left-to-right squeezing pressure, and your shooting hand provides the other 30 percent.

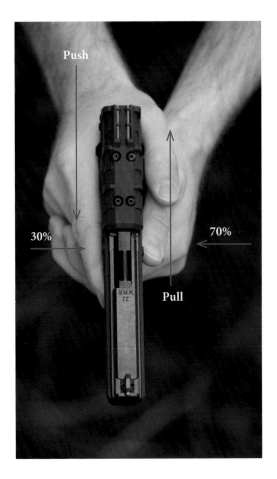

You don't want to have a death grip on the gun, but you obviously don't want to hold it too lightly either. This is something that you will have to play with and figure out what works for you. One simple measure might be to look at your knuckles; if they are turning white, perhaps you might want to try loosening your grip.

Comfort

Whether you're shooting a pistol, rifle, or shotgun, you want to wear comfortable clothes. Generally speaking, tight clothes will not be comfortable. Closed-toe shoes are required at most ranges.

Chapter Summary:

- Determine your eye dominance. If you are cross-dominant, then you can decide whether to shoot right- or left-handed— whichever feels more comfortable.
- Follow the five fundamentals of pistol marksmanship:
  - Aiming: Includes sight alignment and sight picture.
  - Breathing control: Breathe about two-thirds of your air out and then start the trigger-squeeze sequence.
  - Hold control: The process of keeping your sights aligned and on target.
  - Trigger control: A slow, controlled press straight backward. Press, trap, reset.
  - Follow-through: You must maintain your form even after taking the shot. Even after squeezing the trigger, any extraneous movement in your hands and body can throw off your shot.
  - Start shooting in a benchrest position, if possible.
  - Choose one of two shooting stances for beginners: isosceles or Weaver.
- Use the proper pistol grip:
  - Your hands are like a vice, providing isometric tension on the pistol.
  - Proportion the squeeze, with 70 percent in your support hand and 30 percent in your shooting hand.
  - Have firm control of the gun, but not a death grip.
  - Say no to tea cups!

CHAPTER EIGHT

DIAGNOSING PISTOL ACCURACY PROBLEMS AND MALFUNCTIONS

I f you've never fired a pistol before, the first shot you ever take is probably going to be a great one. It'll most likely be right on target, or at least very close to where you were aiming. Then your shots will probably start to go all over the place. Your body may start to anticipate the recoil, and your trigger control may become inconsistent. But don't worry, these are all correctable problems if you know what the problem is and know how to fix it. This chapter will help you master both.

When you're at the range, I recommend shooting three shots at the target, then placing the pistol down to evaluate the results. This will produce a three-shot "group," where the group is how close (or far apart) your shots are. Good shooters are going for tight groups that are in the bull's-eye. If you have tight groups but aren't hitting your target, there may be a problem with the gun's sights, or you might be aiming with your nondominant eye. There could also be other sight-picture issues involved, but the sights and eye dominance are typically the first places to investigate.

Here are some common problems you may see on your target:

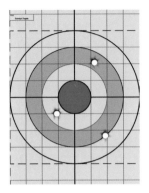

When you first start shooting, your groups may be all over the target. This is normal, as your body and brain are trying all sorts of different things to correct and adjust. By remembering the five fundamentals (aiming, breathing control, trigger control, hold control, and follow-through), you'll have the tools you need to get on target.

I've commonly seen the majority of accuracy issues arise from trigger-control problems. As noted in chapter 7, the trigger must be pulled straight back. Below are some examples of what a target looks like when the trigger is improperly pulled. For left-handed shooters, all diagrams should be flipped on a vertical axis and left/right references reversed.

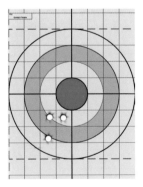

Jerking the trigger—shots
are low and left.

Problem: This group indicates that the shooter is jerking the trigger. This means that, instead of a smooth trigger press, the shooter is pulling the trigger too quickly.

Solution: The shooter should focus on a slowly squeezing the trigger and letting the shot surprise him.

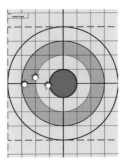

Lateral force applied to trigger—shots are off to the left.

Problem: This group indicates that the shooter is not pulling the trigger straight back and is applying too much pressure on the right side of the trigger.

Solution: While squeezing the trigger, the shooter should focus on trigger-finger pad pressure to ensure pressure is equally spread across the trigger.

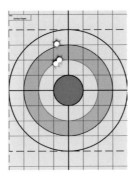

Either the trigger finger flies off the trigger, the shooter is anticipating recoil and raising the gun up as he or she takes the shot, or both.

Problem: The shooter is either not trapping the trigger or not keeping the pistol steady when taking the shot. The action of the trigger finger forcefully coming forward and up will cause the muzzle of the barrel to rise, thereby causing the shots to rise. In the latter problem, the shooter is simply raising the gun up just as he takes the shot.

Solution: For the former problem, make sure to trap the trigger after each shot. For the latter problem, the shooter needs to let the shot surprise him.

Trigger control is one of the most important fundamentals. To improve your trigger control, one of the best suggestions I can offer is dry-fire practice—lots of it. When I'm dry-firing, in certain sessions I like to dedicate the majority of my focus to my trigger-finger pad. It's amazing how such a small body part is so critical to marksmanship. It's small, and therefore it is easy to overlook and get distracted by what your eyes are seeing and what your body is feeling when taking a shot.

Grip problems can also cause accuracy issues. Most common among these are a grip that is too weak, causing the gun to move in your hand when fired. On semiautomatics, this can cause a slide cycling failure and cause a jam.

Breathing problems and fatigue are two other common causes. Remember to be aware of your breath and to break the shot upon exhaling about two-thirds of your air out. It's also fine to lower the gun between shots. Fatigue can set in quickly and affect accuracy.

Hopefully the next time you're working on your pistol skills, these visuals will help you ID the problem and the correct course of action. It's also good to note that many of these problems are hard to identify when you are shooting by yourself. Asking a friend to watch for a particular problem is very useful.

Pistol Malfunctions and How to Resolve Them

You will experience an occasional malfunction caused by your gun, ammo, or technique. At a high level, safety is our top priority in identifying the type of jam or malfunction and what course of action is required to fix the problem.

Sometimes a pistol will jam because it is dirty. Cleaning the pistol is the obvious solution. One thing to note is that, depending on the make and model of your pistol, sometimes too much oil can cause jams or other problems. Consult your owner's manual to see if the manufacturer makes any note of this. I also suggest testing out different CLP (cleaning, lubricating, protecting) oils to see what works best. I can suggest FrogLube as a starting point. More on cleaning in chapter 23.

Other malfunctions can be caused by ammo. It may sound strange to a new shooter, but some guns just don't like certain brands of ammo. Carbon deposits and other fouling from one type of ammo may jam one pistol but work fine in another. I advise testing out other ammo brands to find what works most reliably for your particular gun.

A general condition, called "failure to fire," can occur. This is when you pull the trigger, the hammer drops, and there's only a "click" and no "boom." This can happen to any firearm, including pistols, rifles, and shotguns. It can be caused by an empty chamber (a semiauto can sometimes fail to load a new round) or a spent cartridge in the chamber (common on revolvers, where you lose track of how many shots you've taken).

If you are certain you have a live round in the chamber and you experience a failure to fire, then you need to proceed with caution.

If you are shooting a semiauto pistol, there are specific jams that can occur.

A gun which does not go into battery simply means that the slide has not been seated all the way forward. You'll see a bit of the slide hanging off the back of the frame.

Failure to go into battery is often caused by a round getting improperly fed into the chamber. An oversized cartridge is another potential cause, as is a dirty chamber.

The quick fix is to simply take the palm of your support hand and give the rear of the slide a quick and firm bump. You'll feel and possibly hear the slide seat into place.

Stovepipe

A "stovepipe" is another type of jam.

This is what a stovepipe typically looks like. The brass
can also be offset.

It's called a stovepipe because some folks think it looks like one. You
can often quickly identify a stovepipe jam because the cartridge will be
in your field of view when lining up your sights.

To clear a stovepipe jam, you should tap and rack:

1. Keep your finger off the trigger.

2. Tap the base of the magazine with the palm of your hand. Do this fairly hard. The idea is that the jam may have been caused by an improperly seated magazine; the tap will hopefully reseat it.

3. Rack the slide once, aggressively, with the pistol rotated to the right. The spent round should fall to the ground. (If you do not rotate the pistol while racking, then the spent round will stay put.) A fresh round should now be chambered, and you can bring the pistol back up to continue firing.

What causes a stovepipe? Usually, a shooter is not gripping the pistol tightly enough. so the slide cannot fully eject the shell when cycling. This is colloquially referred to as "limp-wristing" the pistol.

Double-Feed

A "double-feed" is when a spent cartridge fails to eject from the chamber, and the action tries to push a fresh round in.

A double-feed condition.

While firing your pistol, you may not even notice the jam until you pull the trigger and nothing happens. That's normal. With enough practice, you will learn how to feel and see when your gun is jammed. To identify a double-feed, the user must tilt the muzzle up to visually inspect the action. Remember to keep the muzzle pointed in a safe direction while performing the inspection.

To clear a double-feed:

1. Keep your finger off the trigger. Point the pistol in a safe direction.

2. Lock the slide back.

3. Remove the magazine. You may have to use some force to rip it out. Make sure you keep your finger off the trigger when removing the mag.

4. Rack the slide two to three times until you see the spent round get ejected. If the spent round does not come out, lock the slide back and try taking a knife or other sharp object to remove the spent cartridge. Again, make sure you keep the gun pointed in a safe direction while doing this. To the extent possible, also be careful not to scratch your barrel or other parts with your knife.

5. Visually and manually confirm the chamber is empty.

6. Insert a loaded magazine to continue firing, or take a break.

If you experience multiple double-feeds, I suggest first making sure your barrel and pistol are clean. Next, try different ammunition. If neither of those troubleshooting steps work, take your gun to a gunsmith for further inspection.

One type of firing failure requires us to slow down a bit and take caution—ammo failures, which can be dangerous for reasons explained below.

Misfire

A misfire is when the hammer drops on the primer or rim but fails to go off. It can be caused by a faulty or dirty firing pin, or a faulty or a misaligned cartridge. You'll only know what a "proper" strike on the primer looks like for a particular gun and ammo combination after firing at least fifty rounds. A light strike on the primer indicates an issue with the gun that you should then have inspected. Once you know what a normal strike looks like, you can compare it with a misfired round. If you experience multiple misfires, the first and easiest troubleshooting step is to simply change ammo brands to see if the problem persists. If it does, I suggest taking your gun to a repair shop for further investigation.

On the left is an unstruck primer.
On the right is a struck primer.

Hangfire

A hangfire is where the shooter will pull the trigger and it will go click, but then seconds later, the round will go off.

Hangfires can be dangerous because they can at first seem like a misfire. If you experience either one, you should hold the firearm, pointing it in a safe direction, for 30 seconds. You can then rack the slide to eject and chamber a new round, or on a revolver you can cock the hammer to chamber a new round.

To see why hangfires can be so dangerous, watch this YouTube video "Man shoots himself in the head" (almost!): http://goo.gl/fgTo3. This guy broke one of the safety rules, which is to always keep the gun pointed in a safe direction. Had he held the shotgun for 30 seconds in a safe direction, the round would have still gone off and likely surprised him, but he would have stayed safe, which is the number-one priority when handling firearms.

Squib

A squib is when the powder ignition fails to create the normal amount of pressure. Certain squibs make it out of the barrel, but some do not and get stuck in the bore. The dangerous part comes when a shooter has a squib and the bullet remains in the bore, and the shooter than fires another shot and the bullets collide in the bore. This can cause severe injury to the shooter and those in the vicinity, and it can also damage the gun.

Chapter Summary:

- Shoot three-shot groups to gauge your consistency.
- Use the diagrams to troubleshoot accuracy problems.
- Good trigger control is paramount to good accuracy.
- Dry-fire practice will help improve trigger control.
- Malfunctions and jams can be caused by the gun, ammo, or technique.

- Terms:
  - Stovepipe: Spent cartridge gets caught in the slide's ejection port. Tap and rack.
  - Double-feed: Spent cartridge gets caught in the chamber and a fresh round gets fed behind the chambered cartridge. To clear the jam slide lock, strip the mag, and rack the slide two to three times.
  - Misfire: The hammer drops on the primer or rim but fails to go off.
  - Hangfire: The delay between pulling the trigger and the round going off is longer than usual. For misfires and hangfires, it is important to keep the gun pointed in a safe direction and wait 30 seconds in case it is a hangfire.
  - Squib: The powder ignition fails to create the normal amount of pressure.

CHAPTER NINE

BUYING A PISTOL

Now that you have an understanding of how pistols work, think back to your answer to the question about why you want to get involved in shooting. The "right" pistol all depends on your situation. If you are looking for a self-defense gun to keep in your house, a full-sized pistol might work best. But perhaps you are a woman who needs a smaller carry pistol for your purse. Other concealed-carry license holders may wish to carry a pistol in an ankle holster. In that case, a revolver, or subcompact semiautomatic, may be more appropriate.

My First Gun

The author's first gun purchase, a full-size 9mm SIG Sauer P226 pistol.

In 2009, I had been at Google for two years and became financially stable. I had come out of grad school in 2007 with a lot of student debt and wanted to structure my finances so I could have some fun money. For years, I had been thinking about buying a gun but I didn't have the financial resources until starting at Google.

I went to Bay Area Gun Vault in Mountain View, California, one day during a lunch break to go browse and chat. It was sort of love at first sight with the SIG Sauer 9mm P226. I asked if I could hold the pistol, and the sales guy was happy to oblige. Everything just felt right with the P226's ergonomics and aesthetics.

Even though I'm now a Glock guy and shoot a Glock 34 in competition, the P226 will always hold a special place in my heart.

What type of gun you get really depends on your goals. When I purchased my Sig, I wasn't interested in accuracy or the shooting sports. It was really simple—I wanted a cool-looking gun from a reputable company. Just like I've always appreciated Apple products for their form factor and aesthetics, I bring the same approach to firearms and other things I invest in. However, I soon realized that I didn't want my pistol sitting in a safe collecting dust. When *Top Shot* started airing in 2010, it piqued my interest in learning how to become a better marksman.

While I suggest that beginners start off with a .22 pistol, either a semiautomatic or revolver, I obviously didn't take my own advice. However, the first gun I ever shot was a Ruger Single Six .22LR revolver, as I mentioned at the beginning of this book.

The reason why I recommend starting with a .22 is because the ammunition is cheap, which means you'll be able to afford to practice a lot. Secondly, due to the .22's low recoil, new shooters can ingrain really good habits that will benefit them should they graduate to larger calibers. I often practice with a .22LR pistol to retrain or reinforce good trigger control, sight alignment, and sight picture.

There are a variety of .22 pistols out there. Pictured here is a Ruger Mk III (pronounced "mark three") pistol, which is a common entry level pistol. What is really fun is that you can optimize this gun several ways—including adding a new trigger, sights, barrel, and other features—when you get to the point of wanting to improve your gear. Styles of pistols also vary radically. For example, a Volquartsen "Scorpion" model .22 pistol has a very different look compared with a stock Ruger Mk III. It's all part of finding what kind of gun represents your style and meets your particular needs. There's a range in price from a few hundred to thousands of dollars for the majority of pistols available.

The Ruger Mk III. An affordable, entry-level .22 pistol

The author's Volquartsen .22LR pistol, built off a Ruger Mk III platform.

Let's go back to why you want to buy a pistol. If the answer is self-defense, home defense, or both, then I would not recommend a .22 because it lacks the stopping power of a larger round. If you ever need to shoot someone (and hopefully you never do), you want to stop the threat. Larger rounds generally have more stopping power. However, the type of bullet, its weight, and the amount of powder are a few contributing factors. Suggestions vary within the shooting community as to which caliber is best, but a general rule is to use the largest caliber you can accurately control. Many experts agree that .38 or 9mm is the minimum self-defense caliber; however, others might say .32ACP will work just fine.

Other considerations when researching which pistol to purchase is barrel length. Whether on a pistol, shotgun, or rifle, a longer barrel generally translates to the user having an easier time with sight alignment. This is because of a longer sight radius, the distance between the front and rear sights. When researching which pistol barrel length you want to buy, you want to consider that a shorter barrel, and therefore smaller gun, will be easier to conceal if you wish to carry a firearm (check your local and state laws on concealed-carry permits). But with that shorter barrel, you will trade a little bit of accuracy and possibly speed acquiring your target.

A 5-inch barrel .45ACP pistol will often be easier to handle than a 3-inch .45ACP subcompact pistol (Generally speaking, 3 inches is subcompact, 4 inches is compact, and 5 inches or larger is full size). If you go with a .22LR pistol, barrel length will be fairly inconsequential when it comes to recoil management. Also of note is that smaller pistols generally hold fewer rounds than larger ones, depending on the magazine size used.

Once you're done researching some of the details, nothing really replaces going out and handling the firearms you're interested in. Head to your local gun shop or range to check out their selection. The following are some things to look for:

- Can your trigger finger reach the trigger with ease? Remember that you want the middle part of your trigger-finger pad to rest comfortably on the trigger. If the grip is too thick or long, or if your hands are too small or too big for the pistol, you should ask if there are larger or smaller sizes of that particular pistol.

- Ask if you can dry-fire the pistol. How does the trigger feel to you? After testing out multiple triggers, you will start to feel a difference and perhaps a preference for trigger-pull weight (some are heavier than others) and other factors. Your fingers may not have the strength to pull certain triggers or to easily rack a semiauto pistol slide.
- How does the gun feel in your hand? Notice its weight and whether it feels balanced for you.
- What kinds of sights are available? Take aim and look at the sights. Make sure you ask for a safe direction in which to point the pistol.

Finally, nothing replaces test firing. Computer games or video games don't even come close to the real thing. You should not spend your hard-earned money on a pistol unless you've fired that particular model, or at least fired a pistol that is very similar to the one you want to buy. Many gun ranges offer multiple pistol models to rent, and some ranges will even apply your range fees as a discount toward the purchase of a gun if you buy it on the same visit.

Once you've decided on what make and model pistol to buy, prices can vary from shop to shop. Buying a firearm online is also an option. The dealer will ship your firearm to your local federal firearms licensee (FFL) dealer. You'll then go to the FFL to complete your paperwork, background check, and other requirements. One online retailer I can recommend for both great prices and customer service is Bud's Gun Shop (www.BudsGunShop.com). I purchased multiple firearms from Bud's that I then used to train with for *Top Shot*. Not only were the prices the lowest I could find, I really enjoyed working with their customer service.

There are online auction sites where you can also bid on firearms. Many gun owners also post to many gun forums, where there are no shortage of pictures and descriptions. Just like buying anything else online, be prudent about whom you buy things from. A common arrangement is for the seller to allow a buyer to cancel an order upon inspecting the firearm at the FFL. If the seller won't allow this arrangement, buy with care, or continue searching.

Accessories

As a beginner, I recommend sticking with the bare minimum at first and slowly building your gear as you see fit. Gear expenses can add up quickly, and many shooters (including myself) have purchased gear in haste, thinking we needed or wanted it, and now have a collection of stuff we never use.

Here's a short list of pistol accessories you might consider:
- Moon clips (for revolvers)
- Extra magazines (a total of four to six)
- Ammunition speed-loader
- Hard or soft case for storage
- Master Lock 94DSPT trigger lock
- Pistol and magazine holsters (if you are going to get into competitions or carry the pistol concealed)

Chapter Summary:

- Revisit why you want to buy a pistol.
- Start with a .22LR caliber pistol to help engrain good marksmanship fundamentals; 9mm is another good option.
- Gun fit is important. Make sure you can reach the trigger and that the gun feels good in your hands.
- Test-fire multiple pistols.
- Shop prices at gun stores, as well as online.
- Start off with fewer accessories and only buy things you know you'll need. Include safety locks, which offer solid, affordable choices.

CHAPTER TEN

PISTOL ACTIVITIES AND SPORTS

Indoor and Outdoor Ranges

Most pistol shooters are recreational weekend shooters who love to go to the range to relax and enjoy the company of friends and the solitude of being one with their guns. "Plinking" is a general term used to describe a casual, fun shooting environment where one may set up random targets, such as soda pop cans and bottles, fruit, eggs, and other objects. This is a typical occurrence on many private and public outdoor ranges.

Formal indoor ranges generally only allow paper targets, which must be purchased from the store. At both indoor and outdoor ranges, there are safety officers who ensure that shooters are staying safe.

Hunting

Many hunters use pistols to take all sorts of game, from varmints like coyotes to small game, such as squirrel, all the way up to large game, such as feral hogs. There are expert resources, such as the NRA's *The American Hunter* magazine, if you'd like to learn more.

Practical Shooting

When I started shooting, it was at an indoor range at a static line with the typical bench arrangement, with shooting lanes and booths.

I got bored pretty quickly shooting at paper targets standing still in a booth. It wasn't until I started training for *Top Shot* that I discovered the practical-shooting sports world, which includes shooting from a holster and other fun scenarios.

These sports are open to anyone who is of a responsible age, and mental and legal capacity, to use a firearm. It is a fantastic opportunity to shoot with pros and amateurs alike. All pros start off as amateurs, including me. The only way you get better at anything is by surrounding yourself with people better than you.

I started off shooting two different types of disciplines: 1) IDPA and 2) USPSA. Both of these disciplines have shooters wearing holsters for their pistol and magazines who run through courses shooting at cardboard, steel, and moving targets. While IDPA is for pistols only, USPSA and shooting sports sponsored by other organizations, such as the IPSC (International Practical Shooting Confederation), include rifles and shotgun competitions. I remember seeing a match at my local range and didn't know how to get involved. Thankfully, I asked someone, and, to be expected, they were very nice and encouraged me to join.

To get involved in any practical shooting sport, head to that organization's website and search for ranges in your area that organize matches. Contact the range to inquire further about additional training or certifications you may need to obtain. For example, my home range requires a six-hour safe-gun handling course, where you are trained how to shoot safely from a holster and on the move. Only after you complete this course can you compete in IDPA or USPSA matches.

The NRA and USA Shooting, amongst other organizations, also sponsor "bullseye" competitions. Bullseye pistol competitions are shot one-handed and require intense amounts of focus and discipline.

Cowboy action and silhouette competitions are also very popular pistol sports.

One more practical-shooting option is 3-gun shooting, a relatively new shooting sport. In 3-gun shooting, competitors "run and gun," using a pistol, rifle, and shotgun to complete courses of fire. Like many shooting sports, 3-gun shooting is scored on a formula using time and points scores. USPSA and 3-Gun Nation are two organizations that manage 3-gun competitions and can provide more information about this sport.

Keith Garcia is the 2012 3-Gun Nation Champion. Garcia won a $50,000 grand prize, beating out a field of thirty-two competitors. Photo courtesy of James P. Mason / Aegis Atlanta.

Many of these shooting sports have local, sectional, state, regional, national, and international competitions all over the world. There are wonderful travel opportunities to see the world and to meet wonderful people, all while enjoying your firearm with others in sport.

Personal Protection and Home Defense

Many pistol owners decide to purchase a pistol for personal protection and home defense. To carry a concealed pistol in public, the vast majority of states in the United States require a carrying a concealed weapon (CCW) or concealed handgun license (CHL) permit. The name varies depending on which state you live, and there are many other variants.

CCW permits are issued through your county sheriff or law enforcement office. Certain counties have stricter requirements for CCW; depending on where you live, you may not receive approval.

However, many states—such as Utah, Florida, and Nevada—offer non-residents the opportunity to get CCWs after taking a qualified firearms or CCW course, paying an application fee, and going through a background check. Many states will honor other states' CCWs, but others will not. The laws are changing all the time, so I suggest consulting your local and state gun-rights group for further guidance.

Having a pistol in your home for your personal protection is common throughout the United States. Making sure that your pistol is adequately secured from unauthorized persons and children is very important. There is a balance between having your pistol readily available and securing it from access by unauthorized persons. It is up to each individual to strike the right balance for your particular situation and needs.

As mentioned earlier, the caliber of a firearm is important when it comes to defense. While I really hate to talk about guns in any sort of violent manner, the larger the caliber, the more likely you will be successful in taking down an intruder. If you decide to use your pistol for home defense, you really need to think through the ethical and legal consequences of taking another person's life. There are many excellent home-defense courses just for this purpose. The NRA offers two fantastic courses: *Personal Protection In the Home* and *Personal Protection Outside the Home*. Other training institutes offer similar training, so do your own research.

Sometimes, One Shot (or Even Six) Is Not Enough

In January 2013, a mother in Georgia was home with her young children when an intruder broke into the house and forced the mother and her two kids to flee into the attic. When the intruder pursued them into the attic, the mother fired all six shots from her .38 revolver. Five of those shots struck the intruder in the face and neck, but they did not kill him.

Thankfully, his injuries were enough for him to retreat, and he fled in his car. He soon crashed his car and was discovered by sheriff's deputies. The criminal was expected to survive.

One point of this story is that a larger caliber could have assisted in killing the intruder. What if he had been able to continue an attack on the woman and her children even after sustaining five gunshot wounds? And higher ammunition capacity is almost always a good thing when it comes to self-defense.

If you absolutely have to shoot someone, don't shoot them in the leg or shoulder to slow them down or injure them. You shoot to kill. Period. However, in a proper training class, the first thing you learn though is to avoid a confrontation altogether, where fleeing is your first tactic. Putting your pride and ego aside is worth the risk of saving your own life and someone else's.

If fleeing is not an option, talking the assailant down by any means necessary is the next option. Brandishing your weapon is absolutely an option, and verbally announcing you are willing to shoot to kill are additional skills that require training.

Not everyone is capable of taking another person's life, and you should not feel bad if you don't feel capable of doing so. However, I would encourage you to really think through situations where it's "you or them"—and the police or other help are not nearby. What would you do? Make sure you have a plan to keep yourself, your family, and loved ones safe.

This concludes the end of the pistol section of this book. Shooting a pistol well may look easy on TV or video games, but let me tell you, it is much harder than it looks. However, by focusing on the key fundamentals (aiming, breathing control, trigger control, hold control, and follow-through), you will have a huge advantage and learn as quickly as you have time to dedicate to practice.

Next up are rifles and their unique characteristics. As we'll see in the next few chapters, many of the pistol marksmanship fundamentals also apply to rifle marksmanship.

Chapter Summary:

- Indoor and outdoor ranges are great places to practice your pistol skills.
- There are many practical shooting sports where you can have fun with your pistol. Just get out there and try one. There will be fellow gun owners excited to help you get started.
- Pistol hunting is a great way to spend time outdoors and harvest food from the land.
- Using your pistol for personal protection and home defense are common desires. Check out the NRA's course offerings.

PART THREE: RIFLES

CHAPTER ELEVEN

RIFLE BASICS

You may hear rifles and shotguns collectively referred to as "long guns," even though there are distinct differences, as discussed in the next two chapters. While there are many different types of rifles, they share some common parts. The parts and vocabulary for rifles are fairly different than for pistols or shotguns, so we'll go over them here,, starting with the three major assembly groups: stock, action, and barrel.

Bottom firearm is a Houlding Precision AR-15 style rifle in 5.56mm NATO.

Stock

The stock is the part of the rifle that both goes against your shoulder and is held by your shooting hand. Rifle stocks can be made of wood or other synthetic materials. Some stocks are more functional in that the length can be adjusted for comfort, while other stocks are more aesthetic. Some rifle shooters like a stock that is both functional and aesthetically pleasing.

This Volquartsen Custom 10/22 rifle has a beautiful blue wood thumbhole stock. Stocks often come in many colors and variations.

Finding the right stock is important because it is related to your personal comfort. The more comfortable you are, the more relaxed you'll be, which will increase your accuracy. One note is that every stock feels different to everyone, so I am sometimes skeptical if someone says that a certain stock will or won't be good for me. I have to try it myself and make my own decision. The only person who really knows is you, so I highly suggest that you test multiple stocks.

Butt and Butt Pad

The butt is the end of the stock that goes against your shoulder. A butt pad is often a piece of soft rubber that goes on the end of the butt to absorb recoil and make shouldering the rifle more comfortable. Some-times the butt pad is a piece of metal that can increase durability but may be less comfortable. Every rifle is different in that some have butt pads and others do not.

Comb

The comb is the whole top length of the stock where the shooter rests his or her cheek. A good comb will provide a good cheek weld, the contact your cheek makes with the comb.

Pictured with a Houlding Precision AR-15 style rifle. Notice the user's cheek is partially coming over the comb of the stock. This indicates a good cheek weld where the user brings the rifle up to the cheek. Avoid bringing your head down to the comb, which may cause you to tilt your chin down and possibly strain your neck, making aiming more difficult.

Your cheek muscle should be solidly planted on top of the comb. Every-one has different cheek anatomy with different cheekbone heights, so you'll want to ensure you can see your rifle sights. Some stocks have adjustable combs, which will allow the shooter to find the perfect height relative to the sighting system (iron sights or an optic). If the stock has a fixed comb, you may need to try different stocks and sight-ing systems to find the optimal configuration.

Grip

The grip is the part of the stock where the shooting hand goes. There are different types of grips, notably a regular grip and a "pistol grip," the latter being common on the AR-15 platform.

One example of a pistol grip on an AR-15.

A standard grip on a Ruger 10/22 rifle.

Grips have a range of textures, from smooth to rough. The texture can increase a shooter's grip, so find the grip you're most comfortable with.

Opinions vary as to which grip is better, depending on the purpose. Some people say that pistol grips enable them to maneuver the long gun better, or control recoil more effectively, but you'll find an equal number of people who will say the same thing about normal grips. As with most things firearms-related, it's a very personal decision and you should go try different grips to see what works for you. You don't necessarily need to go out and buy every type. If you're at the range and see grips that catch your eye on someone else's gun, most of the time striking up a friendly conversation leads to the owner's letting you check out his or her gear.

Fore End

The fore end is the part of the stock that is underneath the barrel. The support hand often goes there to support the rifle.

However, in some rifles like the AR-15, there is no part of the stock that goes underneath the barrel. Instead, there is a "forearm" that goes around the barrel, which can be grabbed by the support hand.

One forearm style on a Houlding Precision AR-15 style rifle.

A different forearm style on a different Houlding Precision AR-15
style rifle. AR-15 forearms are interchangeable.

There are many types of forearm styles and lengths, especially for
the AR-15 platform. Most AR-15 forearms have attachment points
for flashlights, additional sights, lasers, bayonets, and other accessories. The AR-15 forearm is where many rifle owners love to geek out,
which makes it a popular rifle (in fact, the most popular civilian rifle
in America at the time of this writing).

Barrel

The action is the part of the rifle that contains all the moving parts to
load, unload, and fire. The parts of a rifle barrel are the same as those
of a pistol barrel, as noted on p. 50.

The main difference is that rifle barrels will be much longer than pistol
barrels. While pistol-barrel lengths generally range from 3 to 8 inches,
rifle-barrel lengths generally range from 10 to 30 inches. In the United
States, there are certain restrictions for "short-barreled rifles" (SBRs)
where rifles with barrel lengths shorter than 16 inches must go through
additional paperwork with the Bureau of Alcohol, Tobacco, Firearms,
and Explosives. Certain states prohibit the civilian ownership of SBRs,
so you'll want to check your state laws.

A barrel can be threaded to accept a flash hider, muzzle brake, or suppressor. A flash hider hides the flash produced when the hot gases exit the muzzle. This is important when hunters, law enforcement, military personnel, and other users do not want their position given away by the flash, which is obviously more prominent at night time.

A muzzle brake redirects the hot gases in a way to reduce recoil.

Finally, rifle suppressors are functionally the same as pistol suppressors, as discussed on p. 50.

Action

The action is the part of the rifle through which the bullet travels after the trigger is pulled. A rifle's action is composed of multiple parts that allow the user to load, unload, and shoot. There are a few different types of actions, some of which we'll review here. Opening the action enables the user to load a cartridge into the chamber. Closing the action usually readies the firing pin, so all the user needs to do is aim and pull the trigger. Pulling the trigger drops the firing pin, which strikes the cartridge's primer.

Other parts of the action are magazines and the safety. Magazines are similar to pistol magazines that load subsequent rounds at a faster pace, as opposed to a user manually loading a single round after each shot. Each time the action is opened and closed, a round (spent or unspent) will be ejected and a new one fed into the chamber from the magazine.

Some rifles are magazine-fed, while others are tube-fed. Rifle magazines can be either detachable or nondetachable; it just depends on your specific make and model rifle. Detachable magazines enable the user to reload faster than nondetachable magazines because of the different loading process.

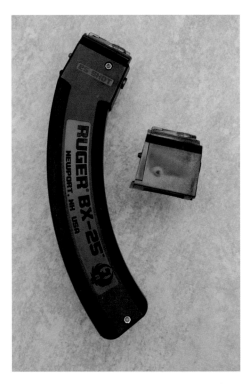

Ruger 10/22 magazines. At left, a twenty-five-round magazine. At right, a ten-round magazine.

AR-15 magazines with twenty-round, thirty-round (Magpul Industries), and sixty-round capacities (SureFire). At far right is a fifty-round magazine drum, by X Products.

Types of Actions

Muzzleloader

A muzzleloader rifle requires the shooter to load a bullet and powder into the muzzle end of the barrel before each shot. Muzzleloader rifles are very similar to muzzleloader pistols with respect to the general loading and firing mechanics. Since muzzleloaders are not as common as the other action types, I won't go into much detail in this book.

However, muzzleloader rifles have a unique place in firearms history and competition, and there is nothing wrong with starting off with one.

Bolt-Action

A bolt-action rifle requires a user to lift the bolt handle up and then pull it back. This sequence will open the action and enable a cartridge to be loaded into the chamber. Many shooters feel a bolt-action rifle is one of the most accurate types of action because you can manually seat the cartridge into the chamber, which can increase accuracy. In comparison, a semiautomatic rifle bolt will quickly push forward and ram a fresh cartridge into the chamber. This fast movement may not align the cartridge's bullet at its maximum center, therefore affecting accuracy.

To load a bolt-action rifle:
1. Make sure to keep your finger off the trigger while pointing the rifle in a safe direction.
2. Grab the bolt handle and swing it up.

Step 2

3. Pull the bolt back until it stops.

Step 3

4. Insert a single round into the chamber. You can either drop it in and let the bolt push the round the rest of the way into the chamber or, for more precision, manually push the round all the way into the chamber, as a lot of rifle shooters like to do. Many shooters believe that a manually seated round will produce more accurate results.

Step 4

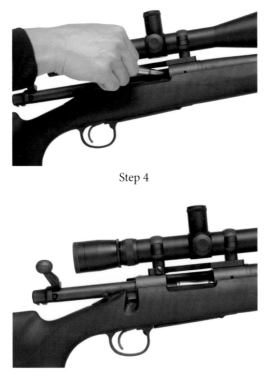

Step 4 in this example shows a round simply resting in the open action.

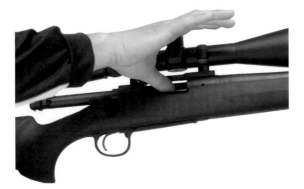

Alternatively, the user can push the round into the chamber, which some shooters believe increases accuracy.

5. Push the bolt forward, and then down to its locked position. The rifle is now ready to be fired.

Step 5

The rifle is now loaded.

If your bolt-action rifle has a fixed magazine, at step 4 you can load it to capacity. To load, you can normally push one round on top of the next.

On a Remington 700 bolt-action rifle, the fixed magazine is located below the chamber. Pictured here is one round already seated in the magazine. To load additional rounds, simply place a round on top of the loaded one and press down until you hear and feel a "click."

If your bolt-action rifle has a detachable magazine, at step 4 insert a loaded magazine. Consult your owner's manual for detailed instructions for your particular rifle.

To unload a bolt-action rifle:
1. Make sure to keep your finger off the trigger.
2. Open and close the bolt (also referred to as "racking" the bolt) repeatedly until all ammunition is out of the rifle.
3. Perform a visual and manual chamber check to confirm the rifle is empty.

Short-Stroking

One thing to note about bolt-action rifles is that, if the user does not fully pull the bolt back when cycling the action, a jam or misfeed can occur. You need to be fairly aggressive when racking the action.

Never Give Up

One of my fondest memories on *Top Shot* was competing with the 1860 Henry lever-action rifle. Chambered in .45 Long Colt, this Civil War–era rifle was a game changer in its day, when Union soldiers could shoot multiple rounds against the Confederacy's single-shot muzzleloaders. The Henry rifle was known as "that damned Yankee rifle they load on Sunday and shoot all week."

The tube-fed 1860 Henry lever-action rifle by Cimarron Firearms.

In one of the closest *Top Shot* elimination challenges ever, I competed against William Bethards, an FBI Specialist and former Marine Corps rifle-team member. Even though neither of us had ever fired a lever-action rifle, I was clearly the inexperienced one.

I fell behind very early in the challenge. The rifle was shooting high for me, so I was supposed to be aiming low to compensate. However, with all the pressure and excitement, I simply forgot and kept putting the front sight right on target, thereby missing high each time. With each miss, William kept taking advantage by knocking his targets down and pulling away with the lead.

About two-thirds of the way into the challenge, I was really behind. I had only six of the fifteen targets down, compared with William's eleven. When the host, Colby Donaldson, noted that I was behind and that I had to "pick up the pace," I felt stressed.

Unbeknownst to me at the time, William was experiencing some problems that opened the door for me to catch up. The last few moments of that challenge were incredible; words just won't do them justice, so I hope you'll watch "The Longest Shot" episode.

Competition is a great way to test the skills we acquire and to see how we stack up against others. I think part of being successful in business, sports, and life is driving through the hard time with relentless focus and energy. Even when I do fall short, I have the peace of mind that I gave it my all and I try to learn as much as I can from the experience.

I know how to handle pressure, and it's a skill I can apply in competition, at work, and in other life situations. This is one example where I tapped my skill set from past experiences and applied it to an active situation. And the next time I'm stressed out I can rely on this *Top Shot* example of how I struggled but also came from behind to win.

Lever-Action

Lever-action rifles are a lot of fun to shoot. They are reminiscent of the cowboy days and were a groundbreaking innovation that enabled a shooter to hold more ammunition in a magazine tube.

A lever-action rifle has a lever connected to a trigger guard, which when pulled down will open the action. Pulling the lever back up will close the action. Rounds are loaded either at the muzzle end of the magazine tube or on the side of the receiver. It is usually one or the either but not both. You'll need to consult your owner's manual for the specifics of your particular lever-action rifle.

To unload a lever-action rifle, while keeping your finger off the trigger, open and close the action repeatedly using the lever until no more cartridges are ejected. To confirm the rifle is empty, a visual and manual chamber check should be performed. Look into the chamber and also place your finger inside to confirm that there is no round present.

Hinge-Action (Break-Action)

A hinge-action, or break-action, rifle is where the barrel hinges away from the breech when a release lever is engaged. The user can load one, two, and sometimes even three rounds, one round per barrel. Most break-action rifles have only one or two barrels, and therefore can only hold one or two rounds, respectively.

Loading a hinge-action rifle is straightforward. While keeping your finger off the trigger, depress the release lever and pull down on the rifle's forearm. Place the round into the chamber, and then close the action. If the rifle has a safety, once that is turned off the rifle is ready to fire.

To unload a hinge-action rifle, while keeping your finger off the trigger, depress the release lever and remove the round.

Semiautomatic

Just like with semiautomatic pistols, semiautomatic rifles fire one round each time the trigger is pulled. With the firing of each shot, the spent cartridge is ejected and the bolt chambers a fresh round from a magazine.

Semiauto rifles can vary in appearance. The Ruger 10/22 (top) and the Houlding AR-15 style rifle (bottom) are both semiauto rifles.

Rifle magazines can vary in shape and size. They can all be disassembled for cleaning and replacing parts. If your magazines ever get dropped in the dirt, dust, mud, or otherwise get dirty, you should take them apart and clean them. If you don't, you risk having a jam the next time you use them.

Magazine capacity laws vary state to state, so make sure to check your local and state laws, or your local gun store. Rifle magazines typically store anywhere from five to thirty rounds. Capacity higher than thirty rounds is also available.

AR magazines.

The AR-15 magazine construction is similar to a typical semiauto pistol magazine. It has a body, follower and follower spring, and a floor plate. Since rifle magazines vary by make and model, consult your owner's manual for further disassembly instructions.

Loading a rifle magazine is often easier than a pistol magazine. You can often simply push a round straight down on the follower, and then subsequent rounds keep going right on top of each preceding round. The magazine lips will keep the round in the magazine, so you do not need to put a lot of downward pressure on the top round to load subsequent rounds as you do with pistol magazines. How do you figure out which way to insert rounds? For most magazines, you will see a lip on one side of the magazine. That's typically where the primer end of the cartridge goes.

To load a semiautomatic rifle, with your finger off the trigger, pull the bolt back and lock it open. Insert a loaded magazine and give it two to three solid taps to make sure it is properly seated. If you fail to perform this step, you risk having the magazine fall out. You can even feel free to pull hard on the magazine to confirm it is seated. Close the action, and you're ready to fire once you turn the safety off. Consult your owner's manual for the specific steps for closing the action on your particular semiauto rifle.

To unload a semiauto rifle, with your finger off the trigger, lock the bolt back. You may or may not eject a cartridge, depending on whether you shot all the rounds in the magazine. Once the bolt is locked, press the magazine release to remove the magazine. This order is important. If you do not lock back the bolt and simply remove the magazine, you could still have a live round in the chamber. If this happens, all you need to do is open the bolt and lock it, but it's safer if you lock the bolt back first.

Perform a visual and manual chamber check to confirm the rifle is empty.

Fully Automatic (Machine Gun)

A fully automatic rifle is capable of rapid fire by holding down the trigger. While many militaries and law enforcement agencies use fully automatic weapons, U.S. civilians who live in certain states can purchase a National Firearms Act tax stamp that will allow them to own fully automatic rifles.

Shooting a Piece of History

The Browning M1919 machine gun, designed by John Browning, was a common fixture in World War II, the Korean War, and Vietnam. The belt-fed M1919 was often mounted on a vehicle, and on *Top Shot* we got to shoot the M1919 mounted to an authentic World War II half-track that served in the European theater. While rolling down a course at 25 mph, we took aim at exploding targets with simulated mortars going off throughout the course.

One thing that's challenging with fully automatic weapons is keeping the gun on target. With every shot, the muzzle rises and pulls off target, so the user must keep the sights on target. Short bursts of three to five rounds are one way to control a fully automatic gun. Oftentimes, your instinct is to hold down the trigger until you go dry. However, you'll see that this approach, while fun, can result in multiple missed shots.

Firing my first machine gun on *Top Shot* was definitely one of my most memorable and thrilling experiences.

Top Shot Season 4 featured an authentic World War II half-track vehicle with a mounted M1919 machine gun. Host Colby Donaldson is at right. Standing at left, from left to right: Greg Littlejohn and Augie Malekovich. Sitting: Kyle Sumpter, Chris Cheng, and Gary Shank. Photo courtesy of HISTORY.

Selective-Fire

A selective-fire rifle has at minimum, a semiautomatic and a fully automatic mode. Many selective-fire rifles also have a three-round burst setting, where each trigger pull will fire three rounds. An NFA tax stamp is also required for qualifying civilians who wish to own a selective-fire rifle.

A number of selective-fire rifles are submachine guns. The "sub" part means that the rifle shoots pistol rounds, such as 9mm, .40, or the relatively new 4.6mm x 30 cartridge. "Subcompact" means that the barrel is short (around 6 inches) and therefore compact.

Shooting a Selective-Fire

I was invited to a private industry event in October 2012 where thirty to forty members of the firearms industry met on a Tennessee ranch to network and shoot a bunch of guns. It was there I got to fire the Heckler & Koch MP7A1, a selective-fire 4.6mm x 30 caliber rifle.

The author with the Hechler & Koch MP7A1 selective-fire rifle.

If anyone remembers the computer game S.W.A.T. from the early 1990s, that was my introduction to the MP5, a popular selective-fire subcompact machinegun chambered in 9mm.

The author with a suppressed Heckler & Koch MP5A2, also selective-fire.

The MP7 is an addition to H&K's subcompact line, which is designed to meet North Atlantic Treaty Organization (NATO) armor-penetrating requirements. The MP7 was a joy to shoot—the 4.6mm round is compact, but it packs a punch. While it is very difficult for U.S. civilians to own a selective-fire weapon, there are a number of gun ranges that allow users to rent them, including some in Las Vegas. However, at of the time of this writing I'm not sure if any of them offer the MP7.

The range officers will give you a brief tutorial on how to operate the machine gun, and oftentimes the experience only lasts 5–10 seconds. They will keep you safe even if you've never fired a gun before.

Shooting a fully automatic firearm is definitely a fun experience I recommend!

There are other types of rifles actions, but as they are less common, I have not included them here.

Safety Mechanisms

Most rifles have a manual safety switch. In the "ON" position, the rifle is supposed to be incapable of firing. In the "OFF" position, the rifle is in a ready-to-fire condition. Variations of this are "S" for "Safe" and "F" for "Fire."

The safety on a Remington 700 rifle.

On an AR-15, the safety usually involves symbols. In this example, the selector is pointing to a picture of a cartridge with an "X" through it. This is the safety "ON" position. To turn the safety off, the user would flip the selector 90 degrees clockwise (twelve o'clock position) to the picture with the cartridge. On selective-fire rifles, the three o'clock position is often a fully automatic setting.

Even if the safety is "ON," you cannot completely rely on it to prevent a rifle from firing. A safety is simply a mechanical part that, like any mechanical part, is prone to failure. Remember safety rule 2: Never cover the muzzle with anything you are not willing to destroy.

Note that not all rifles have a safety, so make sure you consult your user manual.

Chapter Summary

- Parts of a rifle: action, stock, butt, butt pad, comb, grip, forend, barrel.
- Never Give Up!
- Types of actions: bolt-action, lever-action, hinge-action, semiautomatic, fully-automatic, selective-fire.
- Most, but not all, rifles have a safety switch.

CHAPTER TWELVE

RIFLE AMMUNITION AND SIGHTS

Ammunition

At a high level, rifle ammunition shares all the same components of pistol ammo: case, primer, powder, bullet. Centerfire and rimfire ammo is available for rifles. Some ammunition, such as .22LR, and .45 Long Colt, can be used in either pistols or rifles. Centerfire brass is also reloadable, and rifle brass is often more expensive than pistol brass, so it's even more worth saving. The malfunction types (misfire, hangfire, squib) are also the same, and so are the safety procedures.

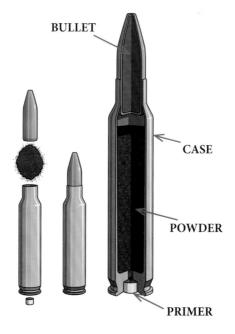

BULLET

CASE

POWDER

PRIMER

Calibers

One of the most confusing things I remember from when I was a new shooter was the plethora of rifle calibers. Some of the more common calibers are .22LR, .223 Remington, and .308 Winchester, but .30-06 (pronounced "thirty aught six") Winchester, .270 Winchester, and .300 AAC Blackout are also popular. There are countless others that I won't go into here. For your first rifle, I suggest .22LR, .223 or .308, since they are popular and widely available. However, if you have a hunting friend or other knowledgeable resource that advises you to get a different caliber, feel free to try it out.

How do you find out what kind of ammunition a rifle accepts? As discussed in the pistol section, a rifle will also have the caliber stamped on the barrel, frame, or both.

Here are some pointers on rifle ammo:
Some rifle calibers have a name after the number part, for example, "Remington" or "Winchester," as mentioned above. These are simply noting the manufacturer or developer of that particular round. Having a similar number in two caliber designations does not make them the same; the other words that make up the designation also indicate differences in caliber. For example, .270 Winchester and .270 Weatherby are totally different calibers. If there is a word after the number, you must make sure the number and word match the caliber for specific rifle. Using the wrong ammo in a firearm is dangerous and can lead to death or injury to you or others in proximity and to damage to your firearm.

In some cases, having different numbers in the designation may not mean a big difference in the caliber; .223 Remington and 5.56x45mm NATO are almost the exact same round. The same goes for .308 Winchester and 7.62x51mm NATO. With respect to guns and ammo, I simply think of NATO as a military organization. Rifle barrels are made for either the civilian imperial measurement or the NATO metric measurement. There is some debate on this, but many people say that civilian ammunition for a .223 barrel can be used in a 5.56 NATO barrel, but not vice versa; other people use 5.56 NATO ammo in a .223 barrel with no problems. There are technical differences between the two rounds, which I won't go into here, but if you would like to learn more I encourage you to search the web or consult with a knowledgeable party. For beginners, I recommend purchasing the exact caliber you see on the barrel of your rifle.

In a caliber such as 5.56x45mm NATO, the number before the "x" is the bullet diameter in millimeters. The number after the "x" is the cartridge length in millimeters.

Some cartridges have two numbers, such as the .30-06 example above. However, a dash in between the numbers does not mean you will always pronounce it as "aught." In this case, the "aught" refers to the zero before the six and, for example, the .45-70 Government round is simply pronounced "forty five seventy." To make things more confusing, the second number after the dash can have different meanings. In .30-06, the "06" simply refers to 1906, when the round was created. In .45-70, the "70" refers to the seventy grains of black powder it was originally designed for. As a beginner, don't worry about making pronunciation mistakes or asking questions if you're not sure about something. Remember, everyone starts out as a newbie, and gun owners are usually more than happy to help if you ask for it.

Sights

Now that we've reviewed a number of common actions, the last part we will discuss is sights. There are three categories: open, aperture, and optical.

Open

Open sights are pretty much a standard item on-out-of-the box rifles. These rifles usually have a rear leaf, notch, or "V" shaped- area, and then a front sight post or bead. There are different ways to align open sights, so you'll want to consult your manual for the proper sight alignment.

The rear sight on a Ruger 10/22 rifle.

Sometimes the sights need to be adjusted, and many times a rear sight can be adjusted for windage (moving the sight left to right) and elevation (moving the sight up and down). We'll discuss zeroing a scope in more detail in a few pages.

Aperture

Apertures are often referred to as "peep" sights, as the rear part of the rifle has a small hole near the action. When you look through an aperture sight, you will see the front sight post. The typical sight alignment is to place the top of the front post in the center of the peep hole.

An aperture sight can normally be adjusted for windage and elevation.

Optical

An optical sight is basically like a small telescope that is mounted to the top of the rifle. Colloquially known as simply a "scope," it magnifies the target to help the user make precise shots.

A Leupold Mark 6 1-6x20mm scope on a Houlding Precision AR-15 style rifle.

There are a number of things about optics that a new shooter should be aware of, as described below.

Reticle

The reticle is what a shooter sees when looking through the scope. A reticle can contain crosshairs, a red dot, or both.

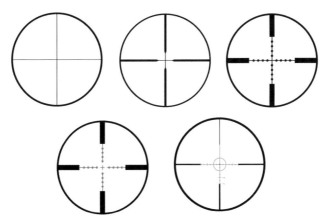

Examples of different reticles, which can vary from simple to complex. Left to right: crosshair, Fine Duplex, Mil Dot, Illuminated Mil Dot, Leupold SPR (Special Purpose Reticle). Photos courtesy of Leupold & Stevens, Inc.

Choosing a reticle is often a combination of how the rifle will be used and personal preference. For example, for action shooters using an AR-15, some prefer a red dot because it enables them to acquire a target quickly. However, for long-distance precision shots, a crosshair reticle would be better, as it has finer details in the reticle. For your first scope, I suggest going simply with a red dot or some sort of crosshair reticle.

Magnification

When looking at scope specifications, you'll see descriptions such as 4x32 ("four by thirty-two") or 1-6x20 ("one to six by twenty").

The number before the "x" is the magnification power. This number describes how many times larger the image will appear—6x is "six power" which means the image will appear six times larger. If there is just one number, then it is a "fixed" magnification and cannot be changed. If there is a dash between two numbers, then the scope is "variable" and can be adjusted by turning a ring on the side where you look through the scope. In our 1-6x example, the scope could zoom in anywhere between one and six power.

The number after the "x" is the objective lens size in millimeters. Sometimes "mm" for millimeters appears at the end; other times it does not. However, this number is always a millimeter measurement. The objective lens is the lens closest to the muzzle. Generally speaking, the larger the objective, the more light will come in and increase visibility, especially at long distances or in lower-light situations.

Base Mounts and Rings

Picatinny (also called M1913, MIL-STD-1913, or rails) and Weaver rail mounts are the two primary base mounts you'll most likely run into. Sometimes there are specific mounts for a specific make and model rifle, but Picatinny and Weaver are the most common.

This Leupold scope is mounted on a Picatinny rail, visible on the right side.

Scope rings go around the scope tube, and then the rings are attached to a rifle mount. Rings come in varying height and tube size. Heights are mostly available in low, medium, high, and super high. You'll need to find the right height primarily based on the objective size of your scope. The objective lens is the scope lens farthest away from your eye. Generally speaking, a larger objective lens will allow more light to enter the scope, thereby making the picture more clear, and easier to see in low-light situations. If you have a large objective size (50mm is on the larger size), low rings are probably not going to work, as there won't be room for the objective. Most ring manufacturers have some sort of chart to help you figure out the right height for your make and model rifle.

The height size is also tied to your facial anatomy and how low or high your cheek sits on the buttstock. I suggest getting the lowest rings possible, and if your cheek is too low on the stock (meaning you cannot clearly see through the scope when you have a solid cheek weld), then you might want to get a different stock that has an adjustable comb.

You can raise the comb to the point where you have a solid cheek weld and can clearly see through the scope. (More on cheek weld as it relates to scopes when we get to talking about rifle stance.)

On tube size, scope tubes are most commonly 30mm or 1-inch—check your scope specs to confirm your tube size.

There are many one-piece base-and-ring combinations available, where the rings are permanently attached to the base.

The main thing for beginners is to get a base that fits your particular rifle make and model. If your rifle has built-in Picatinny or Weaver rails, then you'll want to get rings that can mount to that specific rail type.

Chapter Summary:

- Major rifle parts are stock, barrel, and action.
- Types of actions are bolt-action, lever-action, hinge-action (break-action), semiautomatic, fully automatic, and selective-fire.
- Know your rifle's safety mechanisms.
- Popular rifle ammunition calibers are .22LR, .223, and .308.
- Sight types are open, aperture, and optical.
- Components of optical sights are reticle, magnification (for example, 1-6x20mm), rings, and mounts (Picatinny or Weaver).

CHAPTER THIRTEEN

RIFLE MARKSMANSHIP FUNDAMENTALS

Now that we've reviewed rifle parts, ammunition, and sights and scopes, let's learn about how to shoot a rifle.

As previously mentioned, pistol marksmanship fundamentals —aiming, breathing control, trigger control, hold control, and follow-through—are exactly the same as for a rifle.

There is, however, a difference related to eye dominance. With rifles, you shoulder the rifle on your dominant-eye side. If you are right eye-dominant, you'll shoulder the rifle on your right shoulder, and vice versa. However, notice how this has nothing to do with your dominant hand. You might be right-handed, but left-eye dominant (cross-dominant), so it may seem unnatural for you to do something left-handed. However, I've seen numerous shooters' accuracy improve once they shoulder a rifle on their eye-dominant side. If you're cross-dominant and at all resistant to trying something with your opposite hand, I encourage you to simply try it and see how you like it. At the end of the day, shoot however feels most comfortable for you.

Cheek weld is one concept that deserves a deeper dive when it comes to long guns. Cheek weld, as already defined above, is the idea of solidly placing your cheek in the optimal place on the comb. This optimal location varies for every person and rifle combination. It can vary depending on whether the rifle has iron sights or a scope, the height of the sights, and personal comfort. A good cheek weld will help you become more accurate because you will have the same sight picture each time. This will help you control the rifle and realign faster for subsequent shots.

A good cheek weld is when you can feel the comb pressing underneath your cheek bone. If you see skin, fat, and muscle bulging over the comb, then that's another good sign of a solid cheek weld. With regards to pressure, you want to apply as much pressure on your cheek as is comfortable for you and does not tire you out.

With cheek weld and head alignment, your head should be almost straight up, not tilted to either side. If you shoulder your rifle on your right and find yourself turning your head to look through your left eye, your cross-dominance is causing poor cheek weld.

Notice how the head is level.

Incorrect head alignment. Here the head is canted and the sight picture will be rotated as well. To correct this, the user should straighten her head and press the comb up to her cheek. Also notice that there is a cross-dominant eye issue. The shooter is aiming with her left eye but has the rifle on her right shoulder. The shooter should either mount the rifle on the her left shoulder, or close her left eye and only aim with her right eye.

Sometimes, you won't be able to get a good cheek weld. This is a common occurrence, which is why rifle owners often buy different stocks and accessories to optimize their setup for their particular needs and body type. If you have a rifle scope, sometimes lowering or raising the rings can help, but sometimes getting a different stock is part of the solution. The only way you will find out what works best for you is to try different stocks. Or you can spend a good chunk of change on a custom stock that is fit specifically to you. I might suggest a beginner not go down that road, but if you have the money to spend, go for it!

One last note about cheek-weld placement: You will want to experiment with your cheek location by moving it closer and farther away from the rear sight or scope. If you have a scope, I suggest finding the best spot, using your iron sights first, then mounting the scope on the rail in a position where you can see the full view in the glass. If you see a black hazy ring around the sight picture, then you are either too far or too close. Keep moving your cheek back and forth until you find the right spot.

Each time you bring your rifle up to your face (not your face to the rifle), it should come to the same spot on the comb each time. This takes practice, like anything else. With some hands-on experience, you'll master this skill.

Rifle Stances

Beginners should learn as many of the following stances as they can: benchrest, kneeling, prone, sitting, and standing.

Benchrest

I recommend starting with shooting from a bench, as the rifle will be well supported. Many ranges loan sandbags, wood blocks, and other rifle stands to enhance the shooter's comfort.

Notice that the shooter is simply using his soft case as a rest. The most important thing to note is whether the muzzle is near any objects. The hot gases leaving the muzzle after each shot can easily destroy or ruin range bags or other objects.

Here are some main points for the benchrest position, which are very similar to the pistol benchrest position:
1. Find a solid chair or bench where, ideally, your legs can rest naturally at a 90-degree angle with your feet planted flat on the floor.
2. Sit down and face the target.
3. Find a table or other solid surface where you can place a bag or other support.

4. Rest your elbows on the table.
5. (Optional) Place your support hand palm up on top of the support, then place the rifle forearm on top of your palm. Alternatively, your support hand can rest on your shoulder, your chest, on top of the barrel, or other place that is comfortable for you as long as it is away from the muzzle.
6. Firmly position the buttstock against your shoulder.
7. Sit fairly straight up and continue adding more sandbags or other support until the rifle is level with your line of sight. Don't scrunch your back to go down to the rifle; you want to bring the rifle up to your face.

Kneeling

The main point about kneeling is to have your support-arm elbow on your knee. Some people find it more comfortable to have their elbow on the knee (patella, to be precise) while others like their elbow right above the patella. between the muscle and bone. I believe this is another personal preference area so try different locations. The main idea is that you want your elbow to be stable and comfortable so you can support your rifle.

The shooter can kneel without support or use a tree stump or other object to provide stability.

Prone

Prone means lying on your stomach. Many shooters purchase a shooting mat to protect themselves from cold, wet, hot, or dirty conditions. When positioning yourself into the prone position, it is usually best if you place the rifle down on the ground first, and then go down on your stomach. Trying to get on your stomach while holding the rifle can be difficult for beginners. You want to be aware of your muzzle and make sure you aren't "sweeping" yourself with the muzzle. Sweeping means crossing a part of your body with the muzzle.

The prone position.

Another view of the prone position. Notice how the shooter is low to the ground, which gives him a low profile.

You want to get as low to the ground as possible. Having your legs spread out a bit will provide a base, and I prefer to keep my toes pointed outward. Notice how my body is directly behind the rifle, and not off to one side. The philosophy here is that, after taking a shot, the rifle will come straight back into my shoulder and back onto the target faster. If my body was off to one side, the rifle may not come straight back onto the target as easily.

There is more than one correct prone position, so you can research other variants if you like.

Sitting

Sitting can either be with legs crossed, or with your knees slightly raised up to support your arm. Some shooters like to sit on a foot, as well. Generally speaking, any position where your butt is on the ground is considered a sitting position. It is helpful to practice the sitting position both with and without a rifle support.

One version of a sitting stance.

Standing

Standing is another stance you should practice. Standing stances can vary depending on the exact type of rifle you are using, but there are a few main things to keep in mind.

- Make sure you have solid feet placement, similar to the Weaver feet placement mentioned in the pistol section.

Feet are slightly wider than shoulder width apart and are offset about 45 degrees from the target.

- Where is your support hand resting? Is it closer to the muzzle (see above), or perhaps closer to the magazine well?

The left hand can also be placed on the magazine.

If you need more support, consider the arm-rest standing position. Do the following to set yourself up for this position:

1. Stand with your shoulders pointing 90 degrees away from the target.
2. Place your feet shoulder width apart.
3. Your body weight should be equally distributed on each foot.
4. Pop your hip towards the target, which will create a small resting area for your support-arm elbow to rest in.
5. Bring the rifle up to your face, and your left hand should be as close to the trigger guard as possible.

The arm-rest standing position with an M1 Garand .30-06 rifle

To Chicken Wing, or Not to Chicken Wing?

The "chicken wing" is when your shooting arm elbow is raised up high. Other shooters may opt to relax the elbow, or even tuck it in tight. It really depends on your personal preference and style, the characteristics of the rifle, and any idiosyncrasies of a particular shooting discipline you might be training for—such as the military or competitions.

Personally, I tend not to chicken-wing, as the energy you're expending could be conserved or put towards your focus or other physical needs. However, a chicken wing will create a pocket between your shoulder and pectoral muscle where the buttstock often naturally seats well. Try both ways to figure out what's most comfortable for you.

Regardless of what position you're shooting in, you want to be as relaxed and comfortable as possible. If you feel a part of your body is stressed out, see if you can find a better position and tell your body to relax, or you might just need to keep practicing a particular position until your muscles are used to it. I always need to stretch before going prone because my hip and leg muscles just aren't used to it, and so perhaps stretching or working out certain muscle groups may help.

You might be asking yourself, "Is one of these positions better than the other?" The short answer is "no." It all depends on the situation you're in and what is required. If you're a hunter or a competitive shooter, all of these positions will be helpful. Even if you are just a plinker, changing your position will add variety and keep you interested in new challenges.

Chapter Summary:

- Shoulder the rifle on the same side as your dominant eye.
- Cheek weld is very important. You may need to adjust the comb of your buttstock, or get a new buttstock altogether, to fit your particular facial features.
- Head alignment: Your head should be almost straight up when looking down the sights. Do not tilt your head. If you find yourself tilting your head, it's likely that you are shouldering the rifle on the wrong shoulder and should therefore switch shoulders.
- Bring the rifle up to your face, not your face down to the rifle. The latter will possibly lead to head misalignment and poor cheek weld.
- Stances are benchrest, kneeling, prone, sitting, and standing.

CHAPTER FOURTEEN

BUYING A RIFLE

Similar to the approach with pistols, you'll want to do the same with rifles.

Again, think back to why you want to get involved in shooting. The "right" rifle all depends on your situation. If you are looking for a self-defense rifle to keep in your house, then you should consider your living situation. How close is your closest neighbor? If the answer is anything less than a mile away, I would advise you to research more about calibers, how far each can go, how efficiently each can penetrate walls, and any other characteristics that might make a rifle unsafe to use near neighbors.

Since the possibilities are plentiful, I suggest contacting your local gun shop or other trusted sources for advice for your particular situation.

For plinking, a .22 rifle like a Ruger 10/22 is a fun, affordable, classic rifle.

A Ruger 10/22 rifle with an Oculus scope on a Weaver mount

What is fun about the Ruger 10/22 platform is that you can upgrade the rifle in a piecemeal fashion. I love Volquartsen for their high-quality parts, such as trigger assemblies, barrels, and stocks.

A Volquartsen Custom 10/22 rifle. The blue thumbhole buttstock is a part that can be added on to any Ruger 10/22 rifle. Additional customizations include a match-grade trigger, barrel, and other high-quality parts that increase accuracy and durability.

For hunting, many people prefer a high-powered, bolt-action rifle such as a Remington 700. However, some hunters prefer the AR-15, a modern, semiautomatic sporting rifle.

Houlding Precision produces fantastic, high-quality AR-15 style rifles.

It ultimately comes down to what you want to hunt and then choosing your caliber accordingly. There are plenty of online and offline resources available that specifically cover hunting, so I won't go into any more detail.

For competition, the AR-15 sporting rifle is commonly used in NRA rifle, 3-gun, and USPSA matches, and a number of other competition disciplines. I shoot a Houlding Precision AR-15 style rifle in competition and also use it for target shooting and hunting. There are many AR-15 manufacturers, both big and small. I like to support local companies, and Houlding Precision is a great California company that makes higher end AR-15 style rifles, ready to win out of the box.

CHAPTER FIFTEEN

RIFLE ACTIVITIES AND SPORTS

Competition

USA Shooting, the NRA, the Boy Scouts, Junior Reserve Officers' Training Corps, and other organizations have rifle competitions and programs all across the United States and the world. Competition provides a great opportunity for you to test your skills against the best shooters in your area. Start competing at your local gun club, and, as your skills improve, I highly encourage you to travel to competitions.

There is a big world out there, and some really nice, talented people will be shooting next to you. It's a wonderful community, and it's my hope you'll join us.

Hunting

Hunting with a rifle is like eating with a fork—a common activity that happens daily all around the world. Rifle owners both old and young can participate in hunting, and if you're looking for an enjoyable way to use your rifle, hunting sure is one of them.

To learn more about hunting, I suggest taking a beginning hunter's class and hiring a hunting guide. If you have a knowledgeable friend, that's also a great resource.

Rifle Summary

I hope you've enjoyed learning some rifle basics. There's plenty of additional information out there if you decide to go deeper, including learning about minute of angle (an angular measurement used in shooting), bullet ballistics, the effect of wind, and accessories that are available

PART FOUR: SHOTGUNS

CHAPTER SIXTEEN

SHOTGUN BASICS

As mentioned in the rifle section, shotguns and rifles are both referred to as "long guns." They share the same three basic parts: stock, action, and barrel.

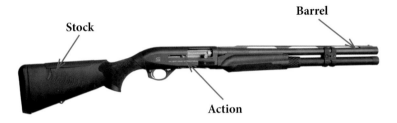

A shotgun stock's parts (butt, comb, grip, forearm) are more or less the same as a rifle.

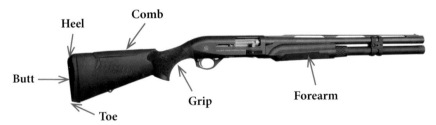

Diagram of a shotgun's parts: butt, heel, toe, comb, and forearm.

However, there are differences that are of more interest to intermediate and advanced shooters. At a high level, there are unique adjustments for a shotgun comb and butt, all depending on the application (for example, trap, skeet, or sporting clays).

Actions

Let's review some common shotgun actions.

Break-Action

A break-action shotgun typically has one or two barrels, and the action "breaks" open so you can load one or two shells, one in each barrel. After the rounds have been fired, the user must break open the action to remove the shells.

On top, a single-barrel break-action shotgun. On bottom, a double-barrel break-action shotgun.

Break-actions are known for their reliability because they have fewer moving parts that could fail, but capacity is a key limitation.

With double-barreled break-actions, there is "over-under" (O/U) or "side-by-side" which describes the barrel placement.

To load a break action shotgun:
1. Make sure your finger is off the trigger.
2. Push the release lever to one side. (For right-handed shotguns, it's usually to the right. Read your owner's manual for details.)
3. With a decent amount of force, "break" both halves open. One small trick is to keep the stock under your armpit or crush it between your arm and the side of your body. As you hold the pressure, you can take your support hand and swing the barrel toward the ground.
4. Load one round per chamber.
5. Place your support hand on the shotgun's forearm while holding the stock with your shooting hand.
6. Make sure your finger is still off the trigger as you swing the forearm up with your support hand to close the action.

To unload a break-action shotgun:
1. Make sure your finger is off the trigger.
2. Push the release lever to one side.
3. Break the shotgun open. Be aware that any rounds (live or spent) may pop out. Either let them fall to the ground, or catch them with your hand. Some shotgun models require you to manually extract the shells.
4. Perform a visual and manual chamber check to confirm that the shotgun is empty.

Pump-Action

A pump-action shotgun has a sliding forearm that manually opens and closes the action after each shot. If the shotgun is loaded, pulling the forearm back will eject the round in the chamber and feed a fresh round from the tubular magazine. Pushing the forearm forward will chamber the new round. The tubular magazine can typically hold anywhere from three to eight rounds. Aftermarket extension options are available for even higher capacity.

A Remington 870 pump-action shotgun. Not only does this shotgun have an after-market extension tube, it also has a forearm integrated flashlight, made by SureFire.

Pump-actions are also known for their reliability because their manual action is prone to fewer jams, and they can store more ammunition than a break-action. Many police departments and military units use pump-action shotguns, such as the Remington 870 and Mossberg 500.

These two pump-action shotgun models in particular are a lot of fun because they are customizable. Flashlights, lasers, ammo pouches, pistol grip stocks, and other accessories are available, and you can replace one or multiple parts at a time. You are only limited by your imagination.

To load a pump-action shotgun:
1. Make sure your finger is off the trigger.
2. If there is a safety, turn it on.
3. If the action is already open, throw one round into the chamber. It will jiggle around—do not worry about this. When you close the action by pushing the forearm forward, the bolt will seat the round in the chamber. If the action is closed, you can either open the chamber by pressing the release lever while pulling the forearm back, or you can just move on to step 3. The release lever is

usually near the trigger, but the location can differ, depending on the model of the shotgun. Consult your owner's manual for more details.

4. In front of the trigger guard will be the loading gate to the magazine tube. Load the magazine tube by pushing each shell up and forward. Push forward until you hear and feel a "click," which signifies that the round is in. Be careful; on some models, you can catch your thumb on the way out. Repeat until the tube is full.

5. If you loaded a round in step 2, then the shotgun is ready to fire once the safety is turned off. If you did not load a round in step 2, then you will want to pump the shotgun to cycle one round from the tube into the chamber.

To unload a pump-action shotgun:

1. Make sure your finger is off the trigger.
2. If there is a safety, turn it on.
3. Depress the release lever while simultaneously pumping the shotgun's forearm. Make sure you do not "short stroke" the forearm, which will cause a jam. Be aggressive in pulling the forearm back and pushing it forward.
4. Keep pumping the shotgun until it is unloaded. Perform a visual and manual chamber check to confirm.

Semiautomatic

A semiautomatic shotgun is magazine-fed and fires a single shot each time the trigger is pulled. Each shot propels the bolt to the rear while ejecting the spent cartridge and resetting the trigger. The user can simply keep pulling the trigger until the gun is out of ammunition. The tubular magazine is functionally the same on a semiauto shotgun as one on a pump-action shotgun. The vast majority of magazines are fixed tubes, but there a few detachable magazines.

A Benelli Vinci semiautomatic 12-gauge shotgun. The camouflage design makes it a great hunting shotgun.

A Mossberg 930 semiautomatic 12-gauge shotgun, modified by Salient Arms International.

Salient Arms International

I was first introduced to Salient Arms International while watching *Top Shot* Season 3. I loved the look of the custom work they did to the Glock 34 pistol, and I knew I really wanted to get a gun done up by them. They also do shotguns, which more than pleased me.

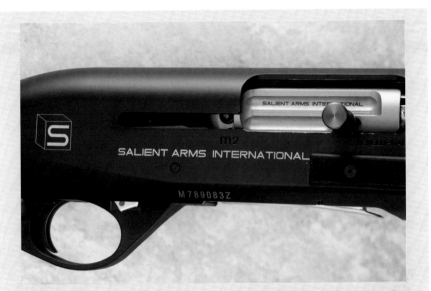

A Benelli M2 semiautomatic 12-gauge shotgun, modified by Salient Arms International.

If you decide to customize your shotgun, or any gun for that matter, there are some purely cosmetic things you can do as well as options that enhance usability. Above is a Benelli M2 shotgun that was modified by Salient in the following ways:

- The bolt was lightened to enable the shotgun to cycle faster in order to keep up with rapid fire.
- The gold ion-bonded bolt increases durability.
- The loading gate is opened up and polished to enable smoother and faster reloads.
- The charging handle is oversized, which allows the user to quickly and easily grasp it.
- The bolt release is oversized, which allows the user to quickly and easily locate it.
- The trigger adjustment has slack taken out and trigger weight is lightened.

Numerous other internal and external enhancements are available as well, all of which you can pick and choose from.

What has been so cool about my experience is that I went from a *Top Shot* fan watching the competition on TV and drooling over Salient's guns, to the *Top Shot* champion who is now sponsored by Salient. I love the work they do and am proud to be associated with them. It's been such a fun career shift to go from computers to guns!

Semiautomatic shotguns are known for their shooting speed, as the user does not need to pump the action in between shots. However, these shotguns are more particular about the type of ammunition used in them, so the user will need to test out different types to make sure the bolt will reliably cycle.

To load a semiauto shotgun:
1. Make sure your finger is off the trigger.
2. If there is a safety, turn it on.
3. If the action is already open, throw one round into the chamber. It will jiggle around—do not worry about this. When you close the action by pushing the bolt release button, the bolt will seat the round in the chamber. If the action is closed, you can either open the chamber by pressing the release lever while pulling the charging handle back, or you can just move on to step 3.

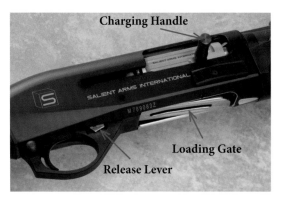

4. In front of the trigger guard is the loading gate to the magazine tube. Load the magazine tube by pushing each shell up and forward.

Push forward until you hear and feel a "click," which signifies that the round is in. Be careful—on some models, you can catch your thumb on the way out. Repeat until the tube is full.

5. If you loaded a round in step 2, the shotgun is ready to fire once the safety is turned off. If you did not load a round in step 2, then you will want to rack the action using the charging handle to cycle one round from the tube into the chamber. To rack the action, use the charging handle to pull the bolt all the way back and then let go of the handle. The spring-loaded tension will do the rest of the work for you.

Barrel

The last part of a shotgun is the barrel, and here's where a shotgun greatly differs from a rifle.

Let's start off with the equivalent of pistol and rifle caliber, which is called "gauge" or "bore" in the shotgun world. The main gauges are 12 and 20. The smaller the number, the larger the round. Then there's .410 bore, which is even smaller than 20 gauge. From a recoil perspective, 12 gauge has the most, then 20 gauge, and then .410 bore. If you would like to learn more about how gauge is measured, other books and the Internet have plenty of information.

12-gauge, 20-gauge, and .410-bore shells.

We'll dive more into ammunition in the next section.

Shotgun barrels also have chokes, which are metal tubes that screw into the muzzle end of the shotgun. Chokes constrict the shot coming out of the barrel, and you need different chokes for different applications.

A picture of some chokes and the choke key to screw them in and out of a shotgun muzzle. Chokes are made to fit certain makes and models, so make sure to only buy chokes that properly fit your shotgun.

Here's a list of choke sizes (from most to least tight) and some common uses:

- Extra full: the tightest choke size that is typically used for turkey hunting
- Full: the next-tightest choke that can be used for trap shooting and hunting certain game
- Improved modified: Used in trap shooting and hunting
- Modified: Used in trap shooting and hunting

- Improved cylinder: Used in trap shooting and hunting
- Skeet: Used for skeet shooting

"Cylinder" or "cylinder bore" means there is no choke in the gun.

Which choke to use for hunting depends on exactly what you're hunting. There isn't a hard-and-fast rule that you have to use a particular choke with certain game, and the type of ammunition and the gun you're shooting must be taken into effect, but there are some things to keep in mind. Smaller game, such as rabbits, should not be shot at with a full choke because the dense shot pattern will most likely destroy the meat. A full choke is more appropriate for waterfowl, such as duck and geese.

Patterning is the process of testing different ammunition, choke, and shotgun combinations. To pattern a shotgun, you set up some sort of target, such as a simple piece of paper, and shoot it from a set distance, often between 25 and 40 yards. You then count the number of shot you see on the paper and compare it against expected results for that gauge with that particular choke.

As a beginner, I recommend just focusing on the mechanics of shooting a shotgun. It is important to be aware of chokes and patterning, and once you're comfortable with the basics you can consult another resource for more on chokes and patterning. If you are shooting trap, consider starting off with a less-constricted choke, such as improved cylinder, as the shot pattern will be bigger and can make targets easier to hit. However, the more spread out a shot pattern is, the less likely you are to hit the clay target. It is a tradeoff, and so you'll want to find the best choke, ammo, and shotgun setup for your particular shooting style.

As with pistol and rifle barrels, a shotgun barrel will have its gauge and shell length. (More on shell length on page 188.)

The engraving reads "12 GA. 3"—76mm FOR 2 ½ or 3" SHELLS."

Some shotgun barrels have a "rib," which is a piece of metal that runs atop the barrel. Differing rib heights can aid the shooter depending on the particular usage. For example, in Olympic Double Trap competition, many shotguns have a high rib, which gives the shooter more time to acquire the target before taking the shot. Shotguns may have high ribs, all the way down to flat ribs, or somewhere in between.

This shotgun rib is slightly raised.

The last thing to note about the barrel is that it often has a front sight post, as well as a mid-bead. These two reference points are designed to help the shooter aim the shotgun properly. Note that some shooters opt to completely remove both posts (see the discussion on sight picture on p. 196).

CHAPTER SEVENTEEN

SHOTGUN AMMUNITION

Shotgun ammunition is very different than either pistol or rifle ammunition. We now know that shotgun shells do not have calibers but rather gauge and bore sizes. You may hear experienced shooters ask about "shotgun calibers," but it's good to know the correct nomenclature.

The composition of shotgun ammunition is unique:

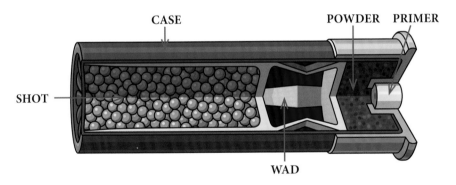

1. Shell: The outer container for all the parts below. Often made of plastic or paper, it is reloadable. Modern shotgun ammo is all centerfire, not rimfire.
2. Primer: Has the same function as in a pistol or rifle primer, but there are specific shotgun shell primers.
3. Powder: The primary energy source that is ignited after the primer is struck by the firing pin.
4. Shot: Small, round, BB-like projectiles, often made of lead or steel. The number of these BBs in a single shell can range from six to over thirteen hundred.

5. Wad: A plastic or fiber part that separates the shot from the powder. The wad forms a seal in the barrel so that the hot gases can uniformly push the shot through the barrel when fired.

Shot Size
Shot size is designated by numbers from #2 to #9. Unlike with gauge, the larger the shot-size number is, the larger the diameter of the shot (BBs) is.

Load
There's also a "load" measurement where various amounts of shot (measured in weight, by the ounce) can be loaded into a shell.

Length
Shells also differ in lengths: 2¾ inch, 3 inch, and 3½ inch. It is very important that you purchase the right-length shells for your shotgun. Remember to check the barrel and frame for the gauge and shell length. If that information is not visible for any reason, consult your owner's manual, or bring your shotgun to a professional for evaluation.

Type
There are three types of shotgun ammunition: birdshot, buckshot, and slugs.

Birdshot, buckshot, and slugs.

Birdshot is used in all shotgun sports, including trap, skeet, sporting clays, and 3-gun competitions, as do other shotgun sports (3-gun also uses buckshot and slugs).

Buckshot is similar to birdshot, except that the BBs are larger. Nomenclature for buckshot is typically "00 buckshot" (pronounced "double-aught buckshot") or "000 buckshot" ("triple-aught buckshot"). There are other types of buckshot, but these are the two main sizes. Buckshot is very common as a home defense round due to the larger-size BBs and their ability to knock a person down .

Finally, slugs are simply large bullets. A slug is a precision round, and, if you are shooting a slug, you want to bring in all the rifle fundamentals, such as focusing on your front sight post as you squeeze the trigger. Some shotgun barrels have rifling (like pistol and rifle barrels). which aid in putting spin on a slug to help remain stability in flight.

Shotgun rounds come in both low- and high-velocity (recoil) varieties, and in many gauges, so finding the correct ammo, shotsize, shotgun, and choke can be a challenge. The "correct" setup is subjective and depends on how you're using the shotgun. Since this book is designed to give you only a high-level overview of marksmanship and how to handle and use firearms safely, I'll refer you to the those who specialize in hunting, skeet shooting, home defense, or other particular gun activities for further guidance on your particular setup.

Chapter Summary:

- The shotgun shares all the same major assembly groups: stock, action, barrel.
- Action types include break-action, pump-action, and semi-automatic.
- Ammunition components are shell, primer, powder, shot, and wad.

- Chokes are used to change the restriction of shot as it leaves the barrel. Different shotgun activities require different-sized chokes.
- Patterning a shotgun is important because it enables you to see the shot distribution at a certain distance. This helps you learn how your shotgun shoots with differing combinations of ammo, choke, and distance.
- Ammunition types are birdshot, buckshot, and slugs.

CHAPTER EIGHTEEN

SHOTGUN MARKSMANSHIP FUNDAMENTALS

Some of the fundamentals we learned with pistols and rifles apply to shotguns, but some shotgun fundamentals differ.

Let's start with some of the similarities.

Eye Dominance

Remember, just like a rifle, your eye dominance determines which shoulder to shoot from. If you are right-eye dominant then you shoulder the shotgun on your right side, vice versa for lefties.

Your dominant hand has nothing to do with which shoulder to use. As already discussed, , a shooter whose dominant-eye side is different than their dominant-hand side is considered cross-dominant.

Shotgun Stances

For the beginner, I recommend that you first learn how to shoot standing, and try prone and bench shooting later. The reason why is that shooting from the bench will not enable you to develop the critical technique you need to learn how to effectively handle a shotgun. On a bench, too much of your body will be relaxed, and the bench will do too much of the work for you. A bench is used to provide stability, which increases accuracy. Since a shotgun is not a precision weapon, we don't need to worry about accuracy with a shotgun as much as we do with a rifle. Sitting down will only enable your upper chest, shoulders, and arms to assist, whereas standing will then include your abs, hips, legs, and feet. Standing enables you take advantage of your full body weight to absorb the recoil and manage the shotgun.

Let me say this right up front: you need to manhandle and control a shotgun. You need to tell it who's boss and be aggressive with almost every aspect of shotgun handling.

To properly shoot a shotgun in the standing position, start in a Weaver stance, as described in the pistol section on p. 90. Put about 65 to 70 percent of your weight on your forward leg (left leg if you are right-handed, vice versa for lefties), which will help you manage the recoil.

Moving up the body to the hips, many new shotgun shooters tend to stand straight up and get knocked off their feet. To partially address this, you want to bend forward 5 to 10 degrees at the waist. This is important, because it will help you control the gun, absorb recoil, and quickly reset for your next shot.

Notice that the upper body is leaning forward to help manage recoil and stabilize the shooter. This solid shooting platform also enables faster follow-up shots.

Note that the degree of bend will vary depending on the game. Trap and skeet shooters tend to stand more upright than 3-gun and action shotgunners.

Another critical part of the shotgun stance is having solid contact with the buttstock and your shoulder. The recoil is going to come straight back at you, and you want your body to absorb it instead of getting hit by it.

To demonstrate getting hit vs, absorbing a force, have someone push your shoulder (where the shotgun would be seated) from 2 inches away with an open palm. Then do it again with the exact force, but this time have the person start with their hand on your shoulder. When there's contact with two objects at the start of the force, the object getting hit will more easily absorb the energy.

Getting Your Shotgun Fitted

I owned my 12-gauge Benelli Vinci shotgun for three years and never had it fitted. I thought I shot fine with it, but it wasn't until after I got a professional fitting that I realized I was compensating for a poor fit. My shooting improved a ton after having the gun fit to my specs. Specifically, the buttstock had to be shaved down. a particular shim was installed to have the buttstock at the correct level so that, when I had a solid cheek weld, I could clearly see down the rib.

Before my fitting, I did not have a solid cheek weld because I had to lift my head up a bit for the front sight to come into view. This was causing all sorts of inconsistency in my trap shooting. I was dedicating a lot of energy to my form when that energy could have gone towards hitting my target.

The length of pull is another measurement a fitter can help you with to make sure your shooting hand is the right distance from your face. Length of pull is the measurement from the back of the trigger to the end of the buttstock. The "correct" length of pull is different for everyone.

A properly fitted shotgun will not only help improve your accuracy (as you'll really be shooting what you're aiming at), but it will help you absorb more recoil and control the gun more effectively. To find a shotgun fitter, contact your local gun shop or range, or consult some shotgun Internet forums.

Think of the shotgun barrel as an extension of your eyes—a line of sight, if you will. New shooters often have a problem with the cheek breaking off the stock after the shot. Most likely this comes from not being used to the recoil, which comes with practice, or shooters break their cheek weld to look above or to the side of the barrel to check the target.

Notice the shooter's cheek and how you can see skin, muscle, and fat coming over the comb of the buttstock. A solid cheek weld is not only crucial for accuracy, but it also enables faster reacquisition of the target after each shot.

When I'm shooting a shotgun, I imagine that my cheek is glued to the buttstock. Perhaps that or some other visualization will help you remember to keep your cheek on the stock.

Just like with cheek weld and head alignment on a rifle, your head should be almost straight up, not tilted to either side. Remember to bring the gun up to your face, and not your face down to the gun. Doing the latter will likely lead to poor cheek weld and a misaligned head placement.

Shotgun Grip

A "standard" shotgun stock is very similar to a "standard" rifle stock in that your shooting hand is placed behind the trigger, where your index finger can naturally reach the trigger.

If your shotgun has a pistol grip, you'll want to grip it exactly like a pistol grip on a rifle.

Your support hand should be placed under the forearm.

Trigger Slap

In shotgun parlance, instead of the trigger squeeze used with pistols and rifles, you "slap" the trigger—which basically means just pulling the darned thing. A shotgun is not a precision firearm like a pistol or rifle (unless you are using a slug, which is covered below). Remember that birdshot is usually hundreds of small metal BBs coming out and forming a circular pattern that increases in diameter the farther the shot goes. Basically, you can be less accurate with birdshot or buckshot, as there are multiple projectiles coming out of the barrel.

When you use slugs, which are a single piece of metal, you need to be precise. Using the "trigger squeeze" framework to hit your mark is appropriate here. Shooting slugs requires a steady hand, so a slower, rifle-style trigger squeeze is appropriate.

With shotguns, finger-pad placement is also not important as it is with pistols and rifles. Typically, your trigger finger touches the trigger around your first knuckle, the one closest to the fingertip. However, feel free to experiment with what's comfortable for you.

One thing to note about trigger slapping though is that don't slap it too hard or else you may end up jerking the trigger and moving the end of the barrel down as the shot comes out. If you are continually missing low on your target, you might be slapping the trigger too hard.

Dry-fire practice is a good way to find the happy medium. You should be able to slap the trigger without dropping the barrel in the process.

Sight Picture

With pistols and rifles, your sight picture should have a hard focus on the front sight. However, with shotguns, your focus is on the target. This relates back to the idea that the shotgun is not a precision firearm (again, unless using a slug). With pistols and rifles, your focus is on the front sight because that is the point when the bullet will leave the barrel, and where the barrel is pointing at that moment will greatly affect its accuracy.

However, since many shotgun sports and other uses require shooting at moving targets, it is more important to be looking at the target when you slap the trigger.

As mentioned earlier, some shooters decide to remove the front sight and the mid-bead (if present). Alternatively, some shooters will take a permanent marker and black out the front sight. Both of these methods are intended to help the shooter focus on the target, instead of the sights.

Lead and Swing-Through

Lead and swing-through are relevant concepts if you are planning to hunt birds or play clay-target sports (particularly skeet or sporting clays). Shooting at moving targets requires lead, which is basically pointing the shotgun ahead of the target. The distance from your target, the type of ammunition you're using, and the speed of the target will determine the proper lead required to hit the target.

Birdshot often moves slower than a pistol or rifle bullet. Remember that with birdshot there are multiple projectiles (BBs) that are leaving the barrel in a circular pattern that expands outward the farther it travels.

The best way I can describe swing-through is that it's similar to follow-through in a baseball swing, a baseball throw, a golf or tennis swing, or a football throw. When the ball leaves your hand or the club or racket makes contact with the ball, the movement of your hand and instrument doesn't stop there; they keep moving. It is the same concept with shooting a shotgun at a moving target. In hunting and many shotgun games, you should be moving the gun with the target. Once you pull the trigger, you should keep the barrel moving at the same speed.

Birdshot creates what is called a "shot string." Imagine that when birdshot leaves a barrel that is not moving, it forms a three-dimensional, cylindrical shape composed of all those BBs. There are gaps in between all those BBs that increase the further the shot string goes out. Now imagine if that barrel is moving while the shot is exiting. After you pull the trigger, the first part of the shot string comes out. As your barrel continues swinging, the shape of the shot string isn't a cylinder but rather like a Slinky toy that is being pushed to one side.

There are many other details to go into at the intermediate and advanced levels, such as fitting your shotgun, what kinds of ammunition to use in which situations, and what kind of chokes to use. I recommend finding some specialized training books, websites, videos, and other sources of information if you are planning to hunt; shoot trap, skeet, or sporting clays; train for home defense; compete, and engage in any other shotgun activities. This beginner's book covers the safe handling and operation of a shotgun, and I've done my best to boil this down to the core essentials to help you focus on the basics.

Chapter Summary:

- Shoulder the shotgun on the same side as your dominant eye.
- Head alignment: Your head should be almost straight up when looking down the sights.
- Cheek weld is a very important concept. You may need to adjust the comb of your buttstock, or get a new buttstock altogether, to fit your particular facial features.
- Stances: Focus on the standing position, but all the same rifle positions can be used for a shotgun.
- Gun fit is important for accuracy and comfort. Find someone who does custom gun fitting.
- Slap the trigger.
- Sight picture: Your sight picture is always a focus on the target.
- Lead: Shoot in front of the target's path.
- Swing-through: When shooting at a moving target, continue to move the barrel after the shot.
- A shot string is a three-dimensional cylindrical pattern of all the birdshot when it is fired from a shotgun.

CHAPTER NINETEEN

BUYING A SHOTGUN

Once again, let's go back to your answer to why you want to get involved in shooting. The "right" shotgun all depends on your situation. For home defense, personally I am a fan of a pump-action shotgun with 00 ("double-aught") buckshot. I like pump-action for its reliability, high-capacity, and simplicity, and 00 buckshot is a generally thought to be a good home-defense round, as it is less likely to punch through walls and create collateral damage. But perhaps you might consider a semiautomatic shotgun; it all depends on a number of factors (which are for another book).

For trap, skeet, and sporting clays, a break-action side-by-side or over-under are generally your main options.

With regards to caliber, I suggest 12 or 20 gauge for the beginner. Even though .410 bore is smaller and has less recoil, it is considered a caliber for experts, as the pattern is smaller and therefore makes it harder to hit clays. However, if you do not plan on shooting at clays and just want to shoot at paper targets, then .410 will work just fine.

With respect to home defense, 12 or 20 gauge is typically more appropriate, as either have more stopping power compared with .410 bore. However, at the end of the day, you should shoot the most powerful gauge where you will get accurate hits. There is no sense shooting a 12-gauge shotgun if you can't hit your target.

Shotguns can cost anywhere from a few hundred dollars all the way into the thousands of dollars. As a general principle, I always say buy the best you can afford because you get what you will pay for. Another general principle is to decide how often you plan to use the item, and pay accordingly. If you're interested in just trying a shotgun, perhaps just go rent a few or go to the range with some friends to try their shotguns.

But if you want to join the hundreds of thousands of shotgun owners around the world, I encourage you to join us.

CHAPTER TWENTY

SHOTGUN ACTIVITIES AND SPORTS

Shotguns, in my opinion, are one of the most versatile firearm platforms available. With so many different types of ammunition (slugs, birdshot, and buckshot) as well as other novelty rounds (Dragon's breath and beanbags, among others), the shotgun is adaptable to many situations.

Clay Bird Games

Skeet

Skeet is a game in which shotgunners take aim at individual clay birds thrown one or two at a time from a "high" house and a "low" house. Eight stations are positioned around a semi-circle field, and shooters take shots from each station.

Diagram of a skeet field.

The United States has some of the best skeet shooters in the world, notably, five-time Olympic medalist Kim Rhode (one gold and one silver, along with two more golds and a bronze in double trap) and two-time Olympic gold-medalist Vincent Hancock. Sergeant Hancock shoots for the US Army Marksmanship Unit.

Five-time Olympic medalist Kim Rhode. Photo courtesy of USA Shooting.

Vincent Hancock shooting skeet in the London 2012 Olympics. He went on to win a gold medal. Photo courtesy of USA Shooting.

There are American and international versions of skeet that are both a lot of fun. The vast majority of skeet shooters use an over-under, break-action shotgun with a 26- to 30-inch barrel.

However, I encourage you to try shooting skeet with whatever shotgun you may have. If you end up liking skeet, you can always purchase a proper skeet shotgun.

Trap

There are many flavors of trap as well, including "Singles" and "doubles" trap in both American and international versions. The general concept is that there is a single "house" that is positioned in front of one to five shooters who are at five stations. The house throws either one or two birds (aka "clays"), and each individual shooter can take one or two shots to destroy the targets.

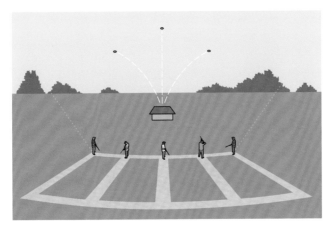

Diagram of an Amateur Trapshooting Association trap field.

With both trap and skeet, the international versions throw the birds much faster, and the shooting sequence is somewhat different. Trap shooters also use an over-under, break-action shotgun with a 30- to 32-inch barrel.

American Glenn Eller is a four-time Olympian who won a gold medal in Men's Double Trap at the 2008 Beijing Olympic Games. Sergeant Eller shoots for the US Army Marksmanship Unit. Photo courtesy of USA Shooting.

The angle the bird is thrown at varies with each trap game, and there are many great resources available if you want to learn more of the details. You should also feel free to try trap with whatever shotgun you may have. Trap is a very fun game that is also good practice for bird hunters during the off-season.

Sporting Clays

The best way to describe sporting clays is that it's like golf with shotguns. Two clay throwers are set up on eighteen different holes (like in golf), and shooters walk or cart to each hole. Each shooter gets two shots to take out two birds. The birds come from every direction.

Shooters typically use an over-under, break-action shotgun, but a semiautomatic or pump shotgun also works fine.

Sporting clays is a very exciting game to play, and I encourage you to check it out.

Hunting

Shotguns are used to hunt many animals, including deer, turkey, rabbit, and many types of birds. Slugs, birdshot, and buckshot are all used, depending on the type of animal being hunted. Pumps, semiautos, and break-actions are all popular choices for hunting.

I suggest consulting a hunting friend, your local gun shop, or your state's department of fish and game for more information on hunting in your area.

PART FIVE:
PUTTING IT ALL TOGETHER

CHAPTER TWENTY-ONE

PRACTICE MAKES PERFECT

As with everything in life, you can't get good at something if you don't practice. Natural skill will only take you so far, and everyone at some point needs to consult with someone better than them. Shooting is no different. I'm still learning a lot, and I proactively seek out advice and training from those who have much more experience than I do. I believe learning is a lifelong pursuit, and the moment you feel like you've learned everything, you're either not pushing hard enough, or perhaps your ego has gotten in the way.

The Learning Mindset

The starting point for learning is wanting to learn. When I taught leadership courses at Google, occasionally there were students who was only there because their manager thought it was a good idea. (I've been in that position, too.) This type of student didn't want to learn and wasn't ready to hear new ideas. From a facilitator's perspective, my approach was to simply present the leadership frameworks and lessons, and engage the skeptical student as equally as I did other students.

Thankfully, the vast majority of students were there to learn. They wanted to learn the content, and they knew what their goals were, along with how the content would help them excel in their jobs. Learning how to shoot is no different. At the beginning of this book, we explored the many reasons why someone would want to learn how to shoot. The list was not exclusive, so perhaps you came up with your own reason. Or maybe you saw a reason you weren't thinking about, and now you've added it to your list of reasons.

Part of a learning mindset is being ready for failure. You will probably fail many times when you start practicing the exercises in this book, but we all fail, and pushing through it is part of learning. Remember that it can take 300–500 repetitions to learn a single fine motor skill. There will be a lot of failure through these reps.

When practicing, you should set specific goals for that particular session. It could be as simple as dissembling your firearm to learn how a particular part works. Or focus on your trigger trapping, sight alignment, or some of other aspect of shooting. The main point is to keep the list very short, one to three goals at most, and structure your practice session so that you're focused on achieving those goals. If you don't have a structure, it can be very easy to get distracted, especially at the range, where I, too, can get distracted and derailed from my practice goals. A good way to stay on track is to shoot with a friend so you can keep each other honest.

How We Learn

Marksmanship is a shooting sport, and I've noted how I've pulled on my baseball background to help improve my marksmanship. To go a little further, I wanted to learn a little bit about kinesiology, the scientific study of human movement and sports psychology. Head football and surfing coach Mark McElroy, of Saddleback College, provided me with his insight.

With regards to motor learning principles, there are four different levels. Imagine football as an example, with the level of difficulty in ascending order:
1. Thrower is throwing at a stationary target from a stationary position.
2. Thrower is throwing at a moving target from a stationary position.
3. Thrower is moving and throwing at a stationary target.
4. Both the thrower and target are moving.

For the beginner marksman, start with the first level, where you are standing still and shooting at a stationary target. Once you master level one, you can then move on to the more difficult levels. Mastering this first level means being able to consistently and repeatedly hit your target at varying distances.

Random vs. Blocked Practice

There are two learning strategies to note, random practice versus blocked practice. Here's what they boil down to:
- Blocked practice: Perform the same action over and over again.
- Random practice: Make lots of changes with each repetition.

For a golfer, an example blocked practice session would be to putt a ball 3 feet from the hole over, and over, and over again. Then perhaps after 5–10 minutes of mastering that distance and the break of the green from the same position, the golfer will move back to 5 feet and perform multiple repetitions.

The random practice session would be the golfer putting once at 3 feet, then moving to a different spot on the green and putting from 8 feet, then moving to 15 feet, and maybe back to 6 feet, all in consecutive putts.

While there are many fans of random practice sessions, it's really a strategy for intermediate to advanced trainees, as adapting to randomness and variance is part of most training.

For the beginner marksman, we should go for blocked practice sessions where you are stationary and shooting at a static target that is perhaps only 3 yards away from you. Keep sending shots until every single shot consistently hits the target. Then you can maybe move it back to 6 yards and perform the same repetitive block.

As a beginner, what you don't want to try is a random practice session where you take 5 shots at 3 yards and then move the target all way out to 15 yards to make it really hard. Then after missing a bunch, you move it back into 7 yards, and so on. If you never mastered the 15-yard practice session, what makes you think you'll master moving all over the place in a random session?

Work your way up to that 15-yard target and beyond through blocked practice sessions. Once you've become somewhat proficient at a particular skill, moving to a random practice session makes more sense.

Self-Visualization

Seeing yourself succeed is a huge part of being successful. I used this technique throughout my entire time on *Top Shot,* where, before a challenge, I'd see myself going through all the motions of loading the weapon, breathing, aligning my sights, getting a solid sight picture, focusing on my front sight, and squeezing the trigger. I'd note my mouth drying up as the adrenaline kicked in. I would even go into further detail, such as feeling the sun's heat or the wind, hearing my teammates and the host narrating the action, and seeing TV cameras and dirt getting kicked up everywhere.

It's about activating all of your senses: sight, hearing, touch, smell, and even taste.

Self-visualization actually goes even further by envisioning your balance and acceleration, your temperature in specific parts of your body (are you sweating, or are your hands shivering, but your body warm?), your kinesthetic sense (where are your body parts in relation to other parts?), pain, and sense of time. It's literally trying to recreate the exact sensation of what it's like being in a particular moment, performing a certain activity or set of activities.

If you want to improve your shooting, before stepping up to the line you have to imagine yourself successfully hitting the target, and diving deeper into the mechanics of what it feels like to grip your firearm, align your sights, take a breath, squeeze the trigger, manage the recoil, smell the burning powder, see the smoke and flash from the muzzle, and, if you're indoors, hear some reverberations, too.

Self-visualization is used by athletes all around the world, and it can definitely be applied to marksmanship, or even work and other hobbies. Whenever I had a particular work project, I would envision myself researching, perhaps even struggling, then succeeding in finding what I needed. I would update a spreadsheet I was using as my project tracker, and I'd envision sending out emails, going to colleagues' offices, and placing phone calls and instant messages for updates. I'd also imagine what success looked like when I was done with the project and what my report might look like.

This is all in my mind's eye, using my imagination to see myself accomplishing the task at hand. If you're open to it, give self-visualization a try the next time you have a chance.

Inverted U Hypothesis

Also known as the Yerkes-Dodson law, the inverted-U hypothesis simply states that there is an optimal relationship between performance and arousal. If you are too aroused, that could translate into nervous energy and a lack of focus. Too little arousal, and you may lack the energy or focus to excel.

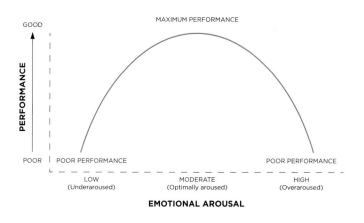

Different activities varying from intellectual concentration to fine motor skills (like shooting) require varying levels of arousal, and naturally it varies from person to person. The main point is to be aware of the fact that your body often needs to be in between being bored and throwing-up nervous to be effective.

Nerves of Steel

Whether I'm giving an important talk or competing, I know that I have to be a little nervous to be at the top of my game. With the stress, my senses and attention get sharpened.

During a 1,500-yard *Top Shot* challenge, we used a long-range sniper rifle to see who could explode a target in the fastest time. I remember not being nervous at all—I was too relaxed. This was bad, as I placed second to last in the challenge. The last place finisher was eliminated, and it could have easily been me. Overconfidence in my ability led to my poor performance in this challenge. In this case, trying to increase my stress could have led to a better performance. It should be noted that calming down when you're too stressed out can be a challenge as well.

Knowing your body and what things you can do to control your stress levels are important. Here are some things I've found that help me: To calm myself down, I take a few deep breaths or go for a quick walk. To increase my stress levels, I jump or run in place or perform some other physical activity, such as push-ups, or I slap myself in the face a few times.

Obviously, there are plenty of other tactics and techniques that can be employed. Each person is different, and you'll need to explore your own solutions.

Most beginner shooters are at the overaroused end of the curve. They're not used to recoil and are generally excited or fear firearms. With practice and becoming familiar with your firearm and the mechanics, your arousal level should drop over time. However, once you move from beginner to intermediate and begin pushing yourself into new, unfamiliar territory, your arousal levels may go back up.

You'll need to find that optimal arousal level that works best for you, as it's different for everyone.

Attentional Focus

Attentional focus is about broadening or narrowing your focus on the task at hand. For example, a baseball player may be walking up to the plate, and the crowd is cheering, or possibly even heckling him. His focus is pretty broad, as he's looking at any men on base, the positions of the defense, the position of the sun, and other factors. But once he's in the batter's box, all of those distractions fall to the side and he's narrowly focused on the pitcher. Once the ball leaves the pitcher's hands, a good batter can see the stitching and determine what kind of movement is about to occur.

As you are practicing marksmanship, you can use this same approach of going from broad to narrow. Before you shoot, take note of your environment, the noise, the lighting, and other external factors, then narrow your focus down to what your body is doing: stance, grip, sight alignment, sight picture, trigger-finger squeeze. Then let the shot surprise you.

The Zone

Finally, athletes often describe "the zone" as a place where mind and body work seamlessly together in an almost unconscious state. This is where we want to be in whatever task we are working on, whether it be shooting, working, or playing. Once you've mastered the core fundamentals of marksmanship, you'll be one step closer to getting in the zone. While there is plenty of further reading on this, all of the concepts mentioned in this chapter feed into helping one get into the zone.

I think part of a winning mindset is also being ready for whatever challenges may await you. Whenever I've been in an unfamiliar, uncomfortable situation at work, sport, or play, I always tell myself that being uncomfortable is actually a good thing. Managing that discomfort level is a skill that will help me throughout my life. "Resilience" is a good word to describe how we have to be strong in the face of adversity. Some people simply ignore the difficulties and press on. Others acknowledge the challenge but gather the strength to move forward. And then there are those who get crushed by the pressure. Pushing through the hard times, staying positive, and keeping a winning mindset are vital to success.

As it relates to shooting or any other activity, being in the zone is simply where you perform all the correct actions in correct form while barely thinking about it. It's almost instinctual. Getting to this state normally takes thousands of hours of practice, building in muscle memory by performing the same tasks over and over again.

Conclusion

Finding a way to press on and perform at your highest potential is a key goal I'm always looking to accomplish. Sports psychology has helped me attain my highest potential both on and off the field, at work, at play, and in life. I hope you will find these frameworks useful when applying them to your life challenges.

CHAPTER TWENTY-TWO

DRY-FIRE PRACTICE

Once you have the winning mindset along with understanding other dynamics around kinesthesiology and sports psychology, it's time to practice. To the range!

However, you might be under the impression that the only way to get good at shooting guns is going to the range and shooting lots of rounds. It's not the only way.

Almost every experienced marksman will tell you that dry-fire practice is essential to improving your skill set. Dry-fire practice is practicing without any live ammunition. Dry-firing is cheap, as you don't need any ammo or any special equipment. While there are many dry-firing accessories, such as snap caps and laser trainers, they are not required for dry-firing.

Dry-firing is particularly useful for practicing the five critical skills we reviewed earlier in the book: 1) aiming (sight picture plus sight alignment) 2) breathing control 3) hold control 4) trigger control and 5) follow-through. One primary thing I always focus on is trying to keep the front sight still while slowly squeezing the trigger. Remember, the average person requires 300–500 repetitions to learn a single fine motor skill.

Setting Up for a Dry-Fire Practice
There are certain procedures to keep in mind when setting up for a dry-fire practice:
- Keep all live ammunition completely out of the room you are practicing in. Make no exceptions to this rule.

- Check and double-check all magazines you plan on using and confirm they are empty.
- Ensure that you have an adequate backstop behind whatever you aim at for dry-fire practice. Even though you will have no ammunition nearby, you still want to follow the Four Rules of Firearms Safety from chapter 2.

Assuming you'll be dry-firing in your home, make sure you close any blinds or curtains that face any streets. You don't want someone seeing you practice and calling out of concern.

Final Safety Tips
Before starting your dry-fire practice:
- Confirm with your eyes and finger that the chamber is empty.
- Do the same with all magazines you'll be using.

A dry-fire session can be as short or as long as you're productive, but most people dry-fire for 5–15 minutes. Try and narrow your focus to one specific objective, such as trapping your trigger. Or if you're working on sight alignment, try transitioning to different targets so you get used to refreshing with each shot.

If you have a semiauto pistol, you'll need to rack the slide after each shot. If you have an empty magazine in the gun, many pistols will go to slide lock if you pull the slide all the way back, but here's a fun tip: You can usually reset the trigger by just pulling the slide back an inch or so. You'll need to experiment with your particular pistol to see where the reset point is located, but it should only take a few racks to find it.

There are also a number of laser systems for dry-fire practice. Some systems are full-replica versions of your gun with installed lasers. You can practice your fundamentals at home or other locations without having to go to a live-fire range. I like to practice transitioning from light switches to the microwave door to other objects at varying distances. Focusing on trigger control is a great use of lasers, as the laser will jump if you have any erratic movements.

The SiRT pistol by Next Level Training does not shoot live ammunition. It fires a laser when the trigger is pressed. The SiRT pistol is an excellent dry-fire option that I use all the time at home.

Some laser systems are a barrel insert you can insert into your real gun, which will make the gun inert. This can be useful if you want to get more hands on time with your actual pistol.

There are laser-targeting systems as well that will light up or produce a sound when you shoot them with a laser.

Dry-fire practice is absolutely essential if you want to improve your marksmanship. Not only will dry-fire practice save you money, but it will give you the increased flexibility of being able to practice at home or other locations on your own schedule.

CHAPTER TWENTY THREE

CLEANING AND MAINTAINING YOUR GUNS

A gun is useless if it doesn't work, and it's definitely no good to you if it gets stolen. In this chapter, we'll talk about cleaning, maintaining, and securing your weapons to make sure they are secured and safe to operate.

Materials for Cleaning and Maintenance

If you're a first-time gun buyer, you will need to have some basic cleaning and maintenance equipment. Below is a list of some core essentials I recommend.

Cleaner, Lubricant, Protectant (CLP)

Once you've removed the layer of carbon grime and other fouling with a solvent, you then need to use a CLP to properly protect and lubricate all the moving parts. There are many CLP brands on the market, but I also use FrogLube for my CLP. It works even better if you apply a heat source, such as a hair dryer, as the heat will help FrogLube permeate the pores in the metal. FrogLube is also 100 percent biodegradable and otherwise environmentally friendly. A FrogLube rep demonstrated this point to me by taking a chunk of the paste and shoving it into his teeth—a pretty impressive demonstration, considering many other CLPs are toxic. Frog-Lube was developed by a U.S. Navy SEAL and is used by hundreds and thousands of troops, law enforcement officers, and regular shooters all around the world. I always make sure to have FrogLube with me.

I use FrogLube, which comes in a paste or liquid and in different sizes, to clean and lube all of my firearms.

Solvent

Solvent is used to break down the carbon fouling that builds up in the barrel, the action, and other parts of the gun. There are many solvent brands on the market, but I've found FrogLube works great.

A Cleaning Mat

When cleaning your gun, you'll be dealing with solvent, CLP, carbon, and other muck, so you need a good-size cleaning mat to protect the surface on which you're doing the cleaning.

Otis Cleaning Kit

Otis makes great cleaning kits that have everything you need: bore brushes, cleaning patches, and other goodies. You'll need to make sure the brushes are sized to the calibers you require. The kit comes with instructions on how to clean pistols, rifles, and shotguns. You can get up to six uses per Otis cleaning patch, which is nice.

Punch Kit and Spare Parts

Depending on what kind of firearm you own, you may want to have some spare parts around in case you need to fix something quickly. Common parts to have on hand are springs, firing pins, and screws. The list is pared down to get you started. There are plenty of other specialized items that you may possibly need, and I recommend looking into that when you buy your gun if you're not sure what they are.

How to Clean Your Firearm

Before cleaning, make sure to do the following:
- Remove all ammunition from the area.
- Wear safety glasses to protect yourself from flying springs, caustic fluids, and other dangers.

Once your cleaning area is prepared, take the following basic cleaning steps:
1. Make sure your firearm is completely unloaded. Do a visual and manual chamber check where you look at and feel the empty chamber.
2. If possible, engage the safety.
3. Depending on the type of firearm you are cleaning, you'll have varying takedown steps. For semiauto pistols, you'll want to separate the slide from the frame and separate the barrel, slide, and springs. For shotguns, you typically just open the action, which is also true for most bolt and break-action rifles. But for many semiauto rifles, such as an AR-15, you'll need to separate the lower and upper receivers and remove the bolt carrier assembly.

A Glock 30S pistol disassembled for cleaning. From top
to bottom: slide, barrel, guide rod and spring, frame.

4. Insert a patch into the patch attachment. Soak the patch with CLP
    and run it two or three times through the barrel, going from cham-
    ber to muzzle each time. If you go the other way, you'll bring more
    debris into the chamber instead of away from it. Let it sit for 2–3
    minutes to let the solvent break down any carbon fouling.

5. While you're waiting, switch out the patch attachment for a brush.
    You'll run the brush through the barrel, breech end first, then out
    toward the muzzle two to three times. The brush will help scrape
    off carbon deposits.

6. Put the patch attachment back on and throw on a fresh cotton
    patch. This time, load it up with CLP and run it through two or
    three times until you stop seeing black fouling on the patches. If
    you're using Otis patches, they are designed to be used six times
    before needing to throw them out. Other patches are generally de-
    signed for one pass before discarding them.

7. Run one or two dry patches through the barrel until they come out
    dry. You may not get patches to come out completely clean, which
    is generally fine.

Other parts of the firearm, such as the slide on a semiautomatic, will also require cleaning. For these parts, you'll need a brush to get in those tight spaces. Start off with some solvent and brush away. Wipe the gun off with a cloth and then apply a light coating of CLP. Many weapons do not require a lot of CLP on the friction parts, and overlubricating can cause jams and malfunctions. Read your gun's instruction manual to see what the manufacturer recommends with respect to the amount of CLP you should use.

If you're cleaning a rifle or shotgun, there may be other parts you will need to clean. On an AR-15, the chamber is one area to focus on, as is the bolt carrier assembly. If you have a tube-fed pump or semiauto shotgun, you should occasionally check the tube for any built-up dirt or grime that could affect the feeding.

Magazines also need to be cleaned from time to time, depending on your shooting environment. If you shoot primarily at an indoor range, you will probably not have to worry about cleaning your mags very often. But if you shoot outdoors, where your mags are getting dropped in dirt, dust, mud, and sand, then you should make mag cleaning a part of your routine.

Magazine cleaning is straightforward: Disassemble the magazine. Take a magazine cleaning brush and run it through. Wipe off any grime on the follower and springs. Reassemble the magazine.

Generally speaking, you should not worry about removing the trigger assembly for cleaning. I do recommend cleaning the area as best as you can with the trigger assembly in place. However, if you have trigger problems with your firearm, you may want to remove and inspect the trigger assembly. Firearms are generally designed for do-it-yourself maintenance, and plenty of instructional videos and websites are available for all popular firearms. If you're not comfortable doing the work yourself, contact a reputable gunsmith.

Once you have cleaned all of the parts, reassemble your firearm and make sure you perform three or four function checks, such as racking the action and dry-firing the gun.

CHAPTER TWENTY-FOUR

ACCESSORIES

This is where things get fun. There is no shortage of accessories you can buy for pistols, shotguns, and rifles; I'll just scratch the surface here to give you an idea of what's out there.

Weapons Lights and Lasers

There is plenty of discussion around whether to have a light or laser mounted to your firearm. It depends on your circumstances and particular needs, so you'll want to consult a knowledgeable party. If you plan to use your firearm for home defense, self-defense, concealed carry, competition, or other situations that might be in low light, this section will help provide you with some options.

SureFire is one company that makes high-quality light and laser systems that are used by law enforcement, militaries, and civilians all around the world. They have standalone flashlights as well as many lights and laser models that can be mounted on pistols, shotguns, and handguns. I have found their products to be rugged and to operate in a reliable manner.

Numerous combinations of lights and laser combos that can be directly mounted onto a pistol, shotgun, and rifle are also available.

A Salient Arms Glock 34 pistol with a SureFire X300 light.

An AR-15 with a Crimson Trace MVF-515R laser and light grip combo.

Another company that focuses on weapon-mounted light and laser systems is Crimson Trace. I have used a number of Crimson Trace's laser and lighting systems on my pistol and AR-15, and I can say that having a light or laser system helps improve my shooting in low-light situations. I competed in a nighttime 3-gun shoot sponsored by Crimson Trace, and I was amazed at how easy and natural shooting with a laser felt to me.

.22 Conversion Kits

A number of pistols and rifles can accept .22 conversion kits. These kits have some swappable pieces—such as the slide, springs, and bolt—that enable you to shoot cheaper .22 ammunition. You have to check whether a specific gun make and model can accept a conversion kit or not; this information can often be found on the manufacturer's website, or through a Google search for third parties that make a kit.

Not only is shooting .22 more affordable, but it can also help you engrain good habits—such as trigger control, sight alignment, and sight picture—using a gun you want to use often. As I mentioned earlier, I recommend training on a dedicated .22 pistol, but that can be expensive for some people. A .22 conversion kit is a wonderful alternative.

Holsters

For civilians, there are three primary reasons why you'd need a holster: for competition, concealed carry, and hunting. Many ranges do not allow civilians to come and shoot from a holster unless you have taken a course or can show proof of experience, such as practical shooting, law enforcement, or military. Some ranges simply do not allow it, period, so you'll want to check on this beforehand.

Drawing a pistol from a holster can be a dangerous movement if you are not familiar with safe gun handling and the particular pistol you're using. This is a skill that should be developed only after getting some experience with the pistol by itself. Take one thing at a time, learn to safely handle and operate the pistol, and then you can start researching holsters.

Holsters are often made of leather, polymer, or neoprene, and several types are available, depending on where you want to carry your pistol. The following are some types of holsters that are available:

- Inside the waistband (IWB): These holsters hold your pistol inside the waistband of your pants. IWB holsters are primarily used for concealing a pistol—remember, depending on what state and county you live in, you will probably need a permit to carry a concealed weapon in public.
- Outside the waistband (OWB): These holsters hold your pistol outside the waistband of your pants. Many uniformed police officers have OWB holsters.
- Belly band: Normally a neoprene band, this wraps around the belly and can store a pistol and oftentimes a magazine or two.
- Ankle: An ankle holster is often used to store a concealed-carry pistol; many police officers use an ankle holster to carry their backup pistol.

CHAPTER TWENTY-FIVE

NEXT STEPS, BEYOND THE BASICS

This book is designed to get you started with learning how to shoot. There is a lot of content intentionally left out to help you focus on the core fundamentals of marksmanship.

Further Reading

Once you are familiar with the fundamentals, there are many specialized books you can read and courses you can take, depending on your interests. They cover, for example, home defense; personal defense; skeet, trap, and sporting clays; and competition shooting (I recommend taking a look at World Champion Julie Golob's book, *Shoot: Your Guide to Shooting and Competition),* such as 3-gun, IDPA, USPSA, long-range rifle, cowboy action, competitive skeet and trap, and many other disciplines. Some activities are specialized for women, youngsters, or seniors.

I highly recommend taking a training course, and there are plenty of options through the NRA's website (training.nra.org), and most likely through your local gun range. The NRA offers basic and advanced certification courses for many firearm types. The organization was founded in 1871 as a training organization and has been refining its curriculum ever since. As an NRA certified instructor, I can affirm that new shooters will receive excellent instruction that will help solidify your understanding and application of marksmanship fundamentals and firearms safety.

Going to the Range

If you've never visited any of your local gun ranges, I highly encourage you to do so. If you're a new shooter, call ahead and say you're a beginner and would like to know about the range, and what you should expect when you arrive. Some ranges are indoor; others are outdoor. Some have a motorized hanger that moves the target toward and away from you, and others have 10–15 minute shooting intervals; at the end of each interval, everyone unloads and stays clear of the shooting benches so the targets can be changed. It all depends, so just ask the range master (the person in charge) about the range's particular protocol.

When you arrive, you'll probably have to sign in and fill out some quick paperwork. You will be asked what firearm you'll be shooting and what kind of ammo you have with you. If you don't have a gun and plan to rent, make sure you know what the shop's rental policy is— some shops don't rent, you have to bring your own gun. Many shops require renters to either already own their own gun or have someone else shooting with you.

If you plan to rent a gun, most ranges require you to purchase their ammo, which may be factory-made or reloaded. They simply want to avoid someone bringing in their personal hand-loaded ammo, which could not only damage or destroy the rental gun, but it could also injure the shooter and bystanders.

I encourage you to ask the range master all the questions you'd like, as it will comfort everyone to know (including yourself) that you understand the range rules and how to safely operate a firearm. A good range master will help you with whatever you need.

Some ranges have multiple target options, in which case the range master will ask you what targets you'd like to shoot at. Some places may only have one target option.

The range is a ton of fun and at some point you are going to want to take pictures of you holding some cool-looking gun to share it on Facebook, Twitter, and the Internet to save it for posterity's sake. I know this because I do it too. However, this can lead to a scenario that I've seen too many times at a range, and that scares the heck out of me: For your picture, you take the gun and turn around 180 degrees to face uprange, that is, away from the targets, and pointing the gun down the safety line at other people. Not only does this violate firearm safety rule 2 (never cover the muzzle with anything you aren't willing to destroy), but I've seen fingers on triggers and actions closed as well. Having a gun, loaded or unloaded, pointed at you is an unsettling experience. As someone who's seen this happen at a range, it's hard to know whether the gun is loaded or not or whether the action is closed and the magazine is inserted.

Acting out this scenario is one quick way to, at a minimum, get a stern warning from a range master and could possibly lead to your getting banned from the range.

If you want to get your picture taken at a range, the proper way is to point the muzzle downrange and just turn your head toward the camera. Whoever is taking the photo can either be right behind you or, better yet, off to one side and behind the firing line. One last thing is to remember is to *keep your finger off the trigger*, and I recommend only taking pictures when a gun is fully unloaded.

Other Places to Shoot

If you are lucky to have access to privately owned land, you could get a clay thrower and some metal targets or bottles and have at it! One of my friends is a member of a gun club here in Northern California where nine families own more than 5,000 acres of land. I went on a hunting trip with him, and during our downtime the seven of us lined up on a porch with shotguns and took aim at clays thrown over a small pond. We did this for close to 45 minutes, and it was a ton of fun.

Once I was exposed to more fun shooting activities away from a static firing line, it really enhanced my enjoyment of firearms.

Another option is land owned by the federal Bureau of Land Management (BLM), which is open to the public. I've been shooting in some fun places in Nevada near Las Vegas and near the site of the Burning Man festival. Our taxes are going towards the maintenance of BLM land, so you should get money's worth.

Taking Professional Courses

There are plenty of fantastic courses you can take to improve your pistol, rifle, and shotgun skills. The NRA has a number of classes you can take for a fee, and you'll be taught by a certified NRA instructor who will reinforce many of the techniques in this book. The National Shooting Sports Foundation also has a "First Shots" program to introduce new shooters to our community and culture.

Other places—such as Gunsite Academy in Arizona and Front Sight near Las Vegas, Nevada—have a large roster of courses you can take. There are a number of other large training schools available as well.

Your local gun range and store will most likely have additional resources and classes to share with you.

Traveling with Firearms

Regardless of whether you are driving, flying, shipping, or transporting your firearm, you are responsible for knowing the local, state, and national laws in countries your firearm will be going through. Caution is advised if you are traveling with firearms to New York City, Washington, D.C., or Chicago, as they have strict gun laws. International travel can sometimes require weeks or months of planning, applying for permits, and making other preparations for bringing firearms, so start your research early.

Since gun laws are constantly changing, consult the appropriate police department or other government agency for detailed information.

Flying

Flying with firearms is actually a fairly straightforward process. I've traveled all across the country through many airports and have become experienced in traveling with firearms.

Your first step should be to check the airline's website with regards to their firearms policy. While each airline has its own policy, it generally looks like this:

1. One checked hard case is allowed that can contain up to five pistols, long guns, or both.
2. The hard case must be locked. It can be put inside another checked item, or the hard case can be checked on its own.
3. Ammunition weighing eleven pounds or less is allowed in either the hard case or in other checked baggage. It must be stored in its original packaging or other container meant for storing ammunition.
4. The weight requirement (generally 50 pounds) for the hard case is applied. Some airlines will charge you for weight over 50 pounds, and other airlines simply won't allow it. If you have ammunition or other accessories, such as empty magazines or scopes, you can move them into a separate checked bag. It's a good idea to weigh your gun case with its items at your local shipping store beforehand.
5. A checked firearm case is treated like any other checked item when it comes to baggage fees. There aren't any special taxes or fees. If you don't have a free baggage allowance, you'll have to pay the regular checked baggage fees for that particular airline.
6. Some airlines require you to check-in at least ninety minutes before your flight. I recommend being at the check-in counter two hours before your flight.

7. No firearms, or firearms parts (including magazines, barrels, receivers, frames), are allowed past security or into a plane's cabin. However, per current Transportation Security Administration (TSA) regulations, rifle and pistol scopes are allowed in carry-on baggage.
8. There is no registration or license required.
9. Curbside check-in is not allowed.

Again, you'll want to check with the specific airline's website for their exact guidelines.

Before you leave home for the airport, make sure your firearm is empty and properly stored in a locked case. You can either have a case with a key or combination lock, and I prefer to *not* use TSA locks, since once the guns are checked by TSA at the counter, there should be no reason for them to examine them again on the way to the plane, or to baggage claim upon arrival. If TSA want to examine my gun case again, they can always locate me at the airport to unlock it.

When you arrive at the airport, here's what the process will look like:
1. Go to the check-in counter with your hard case and identification. You are required to declare that you'd like to check a firearm, and I usually say, "I'd like to declare an unloaded firearm for my checked baggage."
2. The airline will provide a Firearm Declaration tag for you to fill out with your name, flight number, and signature declaring that the firearm is unloaded and secured according to federal regulations.
3. Here's where the process can differ, and it just depends on the airport and the particular airlines:
   a. The airline employee might put your declaration tag in your hard case, put your case on the conveyer belt, tell you to enjoy your flight and send you on your way.
   b. The airline employee might ask you to take your hard case to a TSA screening machine, where you may or may not be asked to open your case for an inspection.

c.   The airline employee might take your case and ask you to wait in a certain area near the counter for a TSA employee to show up.

d.   The airline employee might take your case and ask you to wait in a certain area near the counter; if, after ten minutes or so, no TSA employee shows up, you'll be free to go to security. If the TSA employee shows up and you're not there, then you'll get paged to come back to the counter.

Once you're done with the steps above and before going through security, it is *very* important is to check the pockets in all items of clothing you are wearing or carrying and to check in all bags for any loose ammunition that you may not be aware of. After checking in at the counter your next step is to go through TSA metal detectors. You don't want your trip delayed if TSA finds a live round in your pocket. It's possible that you could be fined or imprisoned for attempting to bring live ammunition aboard an airplane, so this is an important step to take before going through security.

Upon arrival, go to the baggage claim. Depending on the size of your case, your item might be on the regular carousel or it could be in the area for oversized and special items. Keep an eye on both.

Like other airplane baggage, gun cases can get misrouted or lost. I know a few competitors whose guns did not show up for a match on time, but, thanks to the generosity of the shooting community, other shooters are generally quick to loan gear for the gunless shooter. We know that it could happen to any of us, and taking care of each other is one of the great things I love about the shooting community.

All in all, flying with firearms is very manageable as long as you know and follow the rules.

Shipping

If you don't want to bother with the hassle of lugging a gun case to the airport, shipping is always an option. It's best to contact your local gun shop to coordinate the shipping and receiving logistics. If you decide to ship via the US Post Office, you absolutely must contact them ahead of time to discuss your particular situation before bringing any firearm into a post office or even its parking lot, all of which is federal property and may be subject to additional restrictions.

Driving

Transporting firearms in a motor vehicle is another option. In many areas, this includes motorcycles. There are too many combinations firearms transportation laws at the city, county, state, and federal levels to list here, but it's your responsibility to know the laws of every jurisdiction through which you'll be traveling. Certain jurisdictions may require pistols to be locked in a secured box out of reach of the driver, but other jurisdictions may allow loaded long guns within reach of the driver. It really just depends.

Gun laws are constantly changing, so again, make sure you check with all pertinent law enforcement agencies to make sure you are complying with the law.

Public Transportation

Consult the appropriate transportation authority.

Walking

Generally speaking, you can walk with your bagged, unloaded firearm to and from your car, or from your car to the gun range or wherever you plan to legally discharge your firearm.

If you live in the suburbs or other urban area, unless you have a conceal carry permit it's not advised to go run errands with your firearm in a backpack, purse, or other bag. It could be perceived as a method to conceal carry a weapon, which in many counties and states requires a permit through local law enforcement. Violating a conceal-carry law can put you in a really bad situation.

If you live in a rural area, then you might have more-lax laws about walking around with an unloaded, or even loaded, firearm.

The advice for transporting firearms in this chapter is for those that are unloaded and bagged. Walking with a loaded, bagged firearm may not be legal in your area without a proper permit. With regards to walking in public with your firearm, the safest arrangement is to make sure it is unloaded and bagged up. You do not want to attract any unwanted attention, such as a concerned citizen deciding to call the police because you're walking down the city street with a tactical rifle that is not bagged.

All of this will vary depending on where you live, so again, consult your local law enforcement agency for further clarification. Be advised that it can be very challenging to locate accurate information online, and even law enforcement may not be 100 percent up to speed with the current laws.

CHAPTER TWENTY-SIX

CONCLUSION

In August 2011, when I arrived in Los Angeles for *Top Shot*'s Season 4 competition, I didn't know much about guns. Once we moved into the *Top Shot* house and got to know each other, I discovered that my competitors could talk circles around me on the subject. I didn't even recognize many of the terms, tactics, and approaches they discussed, but I listened and learned with eagerness.

I did feel I had one edge—having good marksmanship skills across a variety of platforms. One of the main things that helped me win *Top Shot* was a singular focus on the core essentials of marksmanship. Before starting the competition, for five months I studied everything I have shared with you in this book. However, I knew that winning a shooting competition would come down to one thing: hitting targets. It wouldn't matter if I couldn't tell you the history of a particular gun, its cyclic rate, or list all its parts.

Out of all the information in this book, every time I was thrown into a challenge, I zeroed in on three fundamentals:
- Aiming (sight picture and sight alignment)
- Trigger control
- Breathing control

If you take any technical concepts away from this book, those three are the holy trinity to help you build a strong shooting foundation.

Taking a step back and returning to the first theme of this book, I want to encourage you to think about your entire skill set from work and play. What skills are you good at? Which ones are you not good at? Which ones do you want to develop further, and which ones do you want to let go?

When tackling a problem at hand, I hope you will be able to bring not only your full skills and capabilities to the task but also do so with a positive, can-do attitude where you are the only thing who can possibly stop you.

My entire life I pursued what I thought were the hardest challenges from which I thought I would either learn the most or have the most fun. In high school I really focused on my academics, leadership, and community service. In college, I turned my focus to leadership, building student organizations, community service, and gaining work experience through internships. I am also a musician who played double bass for orchestra and jazz bands for thirteen years. I currently sing for the San Francisco Symphony Chorus. All of these activities I do or did for fun, and to bring as much happiness to my life through exciting experiences. I have also greatly enjoyed sharing those experiences with other people, many of whom have been my really good friends throughout the years.

Following my passion for technology ultimately led me to getting hired at Google, one of my dream companies. In five wonderful years helping to promote a new paradigm around cloud computing, I learned so much from my colleagues and our customers. I worked on a technical support team that fielded direct phone calls and emails from customers experiencing problems. I love to solve problems and bring happiness to people through that channel. It is my hope that the technical shooting skills I've shared with you in this book will bring you happiness and satisfaction by your becoming a better shooter.

I have always wanted to be one of the very best at whatever I am involved in. My strongest critic is me. However, I never feel entitled to be the best; being the best isn't something other people can give to you. It is something you have to earn. You earn it through not only hard work but through disciplined practice and a refinement of your skill set.

What I love about the shooting sports is how objective they are. You either hit the target or you don't. There is no amount of talking or boasting of one's skills that replaces being a good marksman. A common phrase amongst shooters is "Shut up and shoot!"—which I firmly believe in.

Where some people see violence with guns, I see an additional side, where guns protect good people. Whether the police, military, or average civilians such as myself own them, guns are also tools that can help develop confidence in one's abilities, discipline, physical dexterity, and perseverance, amongst other traits and skills.

In closing, I left my job at Google one year ago as of this writing to pursue my professional marksmanship contract with Bass Pro Shops. I have been blessed with so many opportunities to do some amazingly cool things all across the country. I have met some of the friendliest people (the norm in the shooting community), and I've traveled to Bass Pro Shops stores to give autographs and pose for photos, attended industry conventions, and met many of the "who's who" of the firearms world. I went from a nobody to someone whose name and face is now up on posters and such. I've shot more machine guns than I ever thought I'd shoot in a lifetime, and when people ask me what I do for a living I get to say that "I shoot guns for fun."

Only in America could a televised marksmanship competition take someone like me, a random guy who worked in Silicon Valley, and provide this type of a life-changing opportunity. Simply put, I am living the American dream.

Having not grown up deeply entrenched in gun culture, it has been really exciting to embark on the next phase of my journey in life, and I feel so fortunate to share my story with you. It is my hope that my accomplishments will inspire you to go and find *your* next big challenge. Figure out what you need to tackle it, and just do it. Work hard, and your success will be that much sweeter. When you do overcome your next challenge, no need to boast or brag, just hold your head up high, smile, and be proud.

Whether you *Shoot to Win* or shoot for fun (or both), I hope you pursue your passions and win—in life!

AFTERWORD

Welcome to the strange and exciting world of firearms! If you've gotten to this part of the book, you've digested about a decade's worth of gun knowledge, distilled into an easy-to-understand format by someone who, not so very long ago, was in a similar position to yourself. (Or maybe you're reading it in reverse—I do that all the time.) If your only point of reference thus far has been Hollywood and the usual media outlets, you may be experiencing a little head spin at this point. As Chris points out, much of what we read or watch on flickering screens bears little resemblance to reality when it comes to guns.

America has a longstanding and vigorous culture of responsible firearms ownership, which is something that should be cherished, defended, and promoted at every opportunity. By legally owning a firearm, whether you like it or not, you're making a political statement that transcends the stereotypical party boundaries. I'm proud to count as shooting buddies people from all affiliations, orientations, ethnicities, and religions. In some cases, about the only thing we have in common is the fact that we each own these curiously shaped pieces of metal and enjoy using them to launch projectiles with the hope that they connect with something downrange. When you think about it, this a pretty bizarre connection.

Despite this somewhat tenuous link, it's proven to be the basis of long-lasting and rewarding friendships between people who otherwise would never have moved in the same circles. That's an excellent illustration of why it's never a good idea to rely on stereotypes when it comes to guns, people, or life in general. This odd, unifying property of firearms has nothing to do with the actual guns themselves. How can it? They're inanimate objects with no innate properties of their own. Rather, they're a cipher, a symbol of independence and freedom that scares the bejeezus out of petty tyrants and midlevel government functionaries in cheap suits the world over. And that reason alone is worth the price of admission.

When I started shooting, it was in a not particularly permissive environment. England is notorious for its draconian firearms laws, and once the government decided to hang law-abiding gun owners out to dry over the actions of a sociopath, I decided it was time to leave for pastures new and become an American citizen. Before 1920, Britain had zero firearms laws—as in nada, zip, bupkis—and the number of violent crimes could be counted by a first-grader. In less than a lifetime, restrictions on private ownership of firearms was gradually ratcheted up until they reached their logical conclusion of a total ban of fun, useful stuff, such as handguns and semiauto rifles. Oddly enough, the criminal element never got the memo and in the two years after the government confiscated all legally owned handguns, armed crime more than doubled. Conversely, firearm ownership in the United States is currently at an all-time high, and the criminal use of guns has been steadily dropping in the last few decades to a level that hasn't been seen since the 1950s. Do you think there might be a connection there?

Having experienced first-hand what can happen when gun ownership is marginalized and channeled outside of the mainstream, I decided to do everything I could on a personal level to demystify firearms and introduce new people to the legal use of firearms. *Top Shot* fitted nicely with that mission. As a recruiting tool for the firearms community, it's probably brought more people into the fold than any other TV show. It also demonstrated that using guns can be safe, responsible, and above all *fun*, which is probably why the majority of us own them in the first place. So I have to ask a big favor of you, my newly minted, firearm–owning friend. Please, don't keep this awesome knowledge to yourself. The next time you go shooting, take someone else with you and show them what you've learned. Demonstrate the responsibility that comes with exercising your rights, teach them the four rules of gun safety, and then show them the incredible amount of fun you can have just putting holes in stuff.

—Iain Harrison

Iain Harrison with the author at a firearms event.

Iain Harrison is a former British infantry officer who immigrated to the United States in pursuit of the American dream. After a decade of swinging a hammer for a living, he applied to and won a goofy reality TV show, Top Shot, *that launched his career in the firearms industry. To date, he's appeared on every season of* Top Shot, *hosted* Rapid Fire, *a show with absolutely no social value but lots of machine guns, and is the editor in chief of* RECOIL *magazine.*

Harrison continues to compete at national level on the 3-gun, USPSA, and precision rifle circuit, where he's known for taking new shooters under his wing and offering his own performance as an example of what not to do, while giving ill-conceived advice in a difficult-to-understand British accent.

ACKNOWLEDGMENTS

A good work is rarely accomplished by one person. I'd like to start off by first thanking the HISTORY network for making *Top Shot* possible. Zach Behr and Heather DiRubba, in particular, have been great to work with.

Bass Pro Shops is the company that has truly changed my life. Since there aren't many Bass Pro Shops in California, I had never heard of the brand until watching *Top Shot*. It's amazing for me to think that I am now on their Pro Staff, traveling the country representing their brand of enjoying the great outdoors with friends and family. It is a relationship I know I will cherish for the rest of my life. John Acosta and Laura Edwards have been fantastic Bass Pro team members who have made the magic happen.

I have John to thank for introducing me to Kathryn Mennone, who in turn connected me with my editors, Jay Cassell and Lindsey Breuer, all of Skyhorse Publishing. Thank you to Kathryn, Jay, and Lindsey for believing in me and helping make my first book-writing experience such a pleasurable one.

I could not have won *Top Shot* without the support of my bosses and team members at Google. When I explained my *Top Shot* request for six weeks of unpaid leave, my director said, "Chris, I don't completely understand what kind of competition this is, but it sounds like fun. We'll see you when you get back." In typical Google fashion, the company encouraged me to take some time off to go enjoy life outside of work and do something to change the world for the better.

A shout-out to my mentor of many years, David Krane of Google Ventures. I always valued your time, and I thank you for your guidance and advice.

To the *Top Shot* family, I never expected to be welcomed into an extended family. I thought that once *Top Shot* Season 4 aired, I wouldn't see anyone from my own season, let alone any other season. It has been great to meet many of you in person at events on the road and to keep in touch on Facebook. A particular shout-out is in order for the Season 1 cast, who really went out on a limb not knowing if *Top Shot* was going to be a success or not. You guys (and gal) really blazed the trail that led to the show continuing, therefore allowing me an opportunity to change my life. Thank you.

Thank you to Dustin Ellermann and Iain Harrison. I am proud to call you both friends, and I am so thankful for your time and energy for the foreword and afterword.

Thank you to my former Google colleague Tony Lee, who introduced me to Derek Evjenth and David Rudolf at Second Media, a company that owns *The Firearm Blog*, where I have been on staff since July 2012. Thanks to Paul for helping me improve my articles and getting my feet wet in a new role.

The National Rifle Association has been amazing to work with. From Executive Vice President Wayne LaPierre and his assistant, Vanessa Beebe, to Lars Dalseide, John Howard, Samantha Olsen, and Nicole McMahon, I have really enjoyed getting to know all of you.

To NRA Instructors Denise King of Defensive Accuracy (www.DefensiveAccuracy.com) and Ted Lidie of NorCal Firearms Instruction (www.NorCalFi.com), thank you for being such great teachers and role models.

Ronnie Barrett and Ralph Vaughn of Barrett Manufacturing have also been very supportive and welcoming as I started my venture into the firearms industry as a newbie. They are two of the first industry contacts I made after quitting Google.

Gene Hoffman, Brandon Combs, and Jason Davis, collectively of the CalGuns Foundation and the Firearms Policy Coalition, have been great partners in providing me a channel to help promote the shooting sport in California and beyond.

At my home club, the Richmond Rod & Gun Club, thank you to Tom Frenkel, Vince Sargentini, and Brad Engmann (from *Top Shot* Season 1) for welcoming me to the community and for all your help.

I have only improved my shooting capabilities through learning from those smarter and more skilled than me. Craig "Sawman" Sawyer, Robert Vogel, Taran Butler, and Jack Dagger are some of the key people who have really helped up my game.

To Jeff Folloder of the NFA-TCA, thank you for all the machine gun fun! And to Mark McElroy, head football and surf coach at Saddleback College, thank you for all of your insight into sports psychology.

Finally, to Todd of Houlding Precision, Rebecca and Sandy of Master Lock, Captain Larry of FrogLube, Jack of ESP America, Rex of Bud's Gun Shop, and Thomas and May of SureFire, I have thoroughly enjoyed your help and support in making this book a success, and for believing in me and my potential.

To everyone who has met me through *Top Shot* on the HISTORY network, thank you for supporting the show. *Top Shot* represents a celebration of the safe, fun, and responsible usage of firearms. I hope that just like me, watching the show and reading this book will encourage you to go out and shoot!

GLOSSARY

Action: Part of the firearm that contains the moving parts to load, unload, and fire.

Barrel: The part of the firearm through which projectiles travel when the firearm is fired.

Birdshot: A type of shotgun ammunition with small BBs or pellets of varying size. Typically used to shoot clay birds, hunt real birds, and used in competition. Compare with **buckshot**.

Bolt: Piece of the action that manually slides back and forth, ejecting a spent cartridge and replacing it with a new one.

Bore: The hollow part of a firearm barrel.

Breech: End of the barrel closest to the user.

Buckshot: A type of shotgun ammunition with larger BBs or pellets of varying size. Typically used in home-defense, law enforcement, military, and hunting applications. Compare with **birdshot**.

Bullet: Metal projectile that exits the firearm. If the bullet has not been fired, it can be referred to as a cartridge or a round.

Butt (buttstock, stock): Part of a firearm to which the barrel, receiver, and firing mechanism are attached. The end of the stock goes against your shoulder.

Buttpad: Often a piece of soft rubber that goes on the end of the butt to absorb recoil and make shouldering the rifle more comfortable.

Caliber: The diameter of a bullet at its widest part, measured in either inches or millimeters.

Cartridge (shell/round): Holds the bullet, primer, and powder to make a loaded round.

Centerfire ammunition: Ammunition that has a primer in the center of the cartridge's headstamp. Spent cartridges can be reloaded.

Chamber (breech): At the breech end, the area where the cartridge is seated. Chamber can also be used as a verb, as in "chamber a round in the gun," which means to load a round into the chamber.

Cheek weld: On long guns, this is the position during shooting in which your cheek has solid and secure contact with the comb of the buttstock.

Clip: A device that holds ammunition and allows the user to speed-load a firearm. A clip can be quickly identified by its lack of spring, as compared to a magazine.

Comb: The top part of a long gun's stock where the user's cheek rests during shooting.

Cylinder: Part of a firearm that holds the rounds and (depending on the particular gun) cycles either clockwise or counterclock with each cocking of the hammer and/or pull of the trigger.

Double-action: Two actions are performed with each trigger pull: cocking and dropping the hammer/striker.

Follower: In a magazine, a plastic or metal piece that pushes unspent rounds up the magazine body and into the chamber of a firearm.

Forearm/Forend: On long guns, a metal or wooden piece that either partially or completely encloses the barrel. Enables the user to hold the long gun around the barrel for better stability and maneuverability.

Frame: Piece that houses the action parts and, in a semiauto pistol, connects to the slide. The frame is the core pistol part to which everything else (grips, barrel, trigger, slide, cylinder, etc.) is attached.

Full Metal Jacket (FMJ): A way to describe a bullet that is fully covered, or jacketed, in metal. There are other types of bullets that have hollow points, flat noses, etc., and are not completely jacketed. FMJ bullets are very common, often used for target practice and plinking.

Fully-automatic (full-auto): When the user holds the trigger down, the gun will keep firing until there is no more ammunition in the gun.

Gauge: A way to measure shotgun shell sizes. Common sizes are 12-gauge, 20-gauge, and .410. Based off an English measurement system that confuses even seasoned shooters.

Hammer: Part of the firearm that slams down on a cartridge primer.

Hangfire: When the shooter pulls the trigger and there is a click, the primer is hit, but no bang. However, the round unpredictably goes off anywhere between 1–30 seconds later.

Hollow-point: A type of bullet that has a hollowed cavity at the tip. Typically designed to expand upon impact, causing maximum internal damage to the target. Hollow-points have a reduced risk of over-penetrating the target and reduce the risk of collateral damage. Hollow-points are very common in self-defense situations.

Magazine: A device to hold ammunition that allows the user to speed-load a firearm. A magazine can be quickly identified by the existence of a spring pushing a follower.

Misfire: When the hammer drops on the primer or rim but the round fails to go off. A misfire is similar to a hangfire except that a misfire does not result in a discharge.

Muzzle: The end where the bullet leaves the barrel.

Primer: Part of the cartridge that, when struck by the firing pin or hammer, ignites the primary powder charge.

Pump-action: A firearm with a sliding forearm that manually opens and closes the action after each shot.

Receiver: Part of the firearm that houses the moving and operating parts such as the bolt, trigger, magazine port, latches, switches, etc. In pistols, also referred to as the **frame**.

Recoil: The backward action of a firearm upon firing.

Rimfire ammunition: Ammunition that has a primer on the rim of the cartridge's headstamp. Spent cartridges cannot be reloaded.

Safety: A mechanical switch on a firearm that prevents a firearm from discharging. Not all firearms have a safety, and safety mechanisms can fail. **ALWAYS** follow the four rules of safe firearm handling.

Semiautomatic (semiauto): An action or mode in which the user pulls the trigger and only one shot occurs. The user can then repeatedly pull the trigger to fire additional single shots with each pull until there is no more ammunition in the gun.

Sight alignment: The process of aligning the rear sight and front sights.

Sight picture: The view the user sees of the sights on the target.

Sights: Helps the user aim a firearm. Can come in multiple forms such as iron sights, optical, laser, and peep.

Single-action: One action, dropping the hammer/striker, is performed with each trigger squeeze.

Slide: Top part of a pistol that houses the barrel and other parts.

Striker: A spring-loaded firing pin.

Slug: A type of shotgun ammunition that is essentially a large bullet. Can also be a pistol bullet.

Squib: When the powder ignition fails to create the normal amount of pressure, and the bullet may or may not exit the barrel.

Tap and rack: A malfunction clearance procedure in which the user aggressively "taps" the magazine to make sure it is fully seated and then "racks" the slide to clear and chamber a round.

Trigger: Part of the firearm that is pulled to drop the hammer/striker.

Trigger guard: Piece that protects the trigger from accidentally going off from inadvertent bumps, mishandling, etc.

CHRIS CHENG'S GUNS & GEAR

Guns
- 1860 Henry Rifle provided by Cimarron Firearms (www.cimarron-firearms.com)
- Benelli M2 12-gauge Shotgun provided by Bass Pro Shops (www.BassPro.com), modified by Salient Arms International (www.SalientArms.com)
- Glock 34 9mm pistol provided by Bass Pro Shops (www.BassPro.com), modified by Salient Arms International (www.SalientArms.com)
- Houlding Precision AR-15 style rifle provided by Houlding Precision Firearms (www.HouldingPrecision.com)
- Volquartsen .22LR 10/22 rifle provided by Volquartsen Custom (www.Volquartsen.com)
- Volquartsen Scorpion .22LR pistol provided by Volquartsen Custom (www.Volquartsen.com)
- Online firearm shopping available at Bud's Gun Shop (www.BudsGunShop.com)

Gear
- Crimson Trace MVF-515 red laser and light vertical foregrip (www.CrimsonTrace.com)
- ESP America electronic ear protection. Stealth model. (www.ESPAmerica.com)
- Leupold Mark 6 1-6x20mm CMR-W scope provided by Leupold & Stevens (www.Leupold.com)
- SureFire X300 Picatinny rail light (www.SureFire.com)

Accessories
- FrogLube CLP (www.FrogLube.com)
- Master Lock 94DSPT trigger lock (www.MasterLock.com)
- SiRT training pistol by Next Level Training (www.NextLevel-Training.com)

- 10 percent discount code: TS4
- 20 percent discount code for military and law enforcement: TS4LE

Atlatls are available for purchase through Chris Henry (www.PaleoArts.net).

CONTRIBUTORS

Chris Cheng

Chris Cheng is the HISTORY network's *Top Shot* Season 4 champion. He was born and raised in Mission Viejo, California, and attended the University of California, Los Angeles for his B.A. in political science; the Monterey Institute of International Studies for his M.A. in international policy studies; and he holds an Advanced Project Management Certification from Stanford University.

Before winning *Top Shot* Season 4 in May 2012, Cheng worked at Google from 2007 to 2012 in multiple roles: a technical support specialist and manager, a leadership and professional development trainer, and several roles in marketing and sales. Cheng thoroughly enjoyed his time at Google, helping pioneer "cloud computing" before the term became ubiquitous in Silicon Valley. He is an unabashed Apple and Google fanboy.

In addition to the title of "Top Shot," Cheng won a $100,000 cash prize and a professional marksman contract with *Top Shot's* sponsor, Bass Pro Shops. Cheng travels the country competing in 3-gun, USPSA, and IDPA competitions, and appears at Bass Pro Shops stores for special events.

Cheng is part of the NRA News *Commentators* team where he shares his opinions and perspectives on firearms, the Second Amendment, and American culture. Cheng has attended the annual SHOT Show and NRA Annual Meeting for fan appearances and to show his support for the Second Amendment, along with more than 70,000 attendees.

Cheng is a Staff Writer for *The Firearm Blog,* where he reviews firearms and gear, and shares his new experiences in the industry. He is also a range officer and member of the Richmond Rod & Gun Club in Richmond, California. Cheng is a lifetime member of the National Rifle Association and the California Rifle and Pistol Association.

He is a certified NRA pistol, rifle, and shotgun instructor. He was a keynote speaker for the NRA Youth Education Summit in 2013 and has donated autographed Ruger and Volquartsen rifles to support NRA-ILA fundraising efforts. He is also featured in the documentary *Assaulted: Civil Rights Under Fire,* speaking about his support for the Second Amendment.

Cheng has a newfound love and interest in the ethics of hunting as a way of connecting with our food. He is often seen taking San Francisco foodies, chefs, and restaurant owners to the shooting range to share his passion for food and firearms.

Cheng's hobbies and interests include serving as a volunteer baritone singer for the San Francisco Symphony Chorus, serving on the board of directors for the San Francisco Opera BRAVO! Club, as well as cofounding a nonprofit organization, Home for a Home, which aims to bring social responsibility to the real estate industry.

Lastly, Cheng has been a long-time supporter of HIV/AIDS prevention and eradication, as well as lesbian, gay, bisexual, and transgender rights. At UCLA, he was co-chair of the UCLA Dance Marathon, where more than 2,000 people raised $54,000 for pediatric AIDS in a 26-hour dance marathon. At Google, he volunteered for corporate diversity initiatives, and he has ridden his bike 545 miles from San Francisco to Los Angeles three times and personally raised more than $15,000 for HIV/AIDS awareness and treatment for those in need. He has also donated shooting lessons to the Human Rights Campaign and Horizons Foundation annual Gala silent auctions.

When he's not doing those activities, Cheng can be seen connecting with the San Francisco food and drink scene, snowboarding, travelling, and finding the next challenge or adventure in life.

www.TopShotChris.com.

Oleg Volk, Main Photographer

Oleg Volk is a creative director and photographer living in Nashville, TN. Since emigrating from the USSR at age 15, he has concentrated on promoting personal freedoms and, chief among them, the right to keep and bear arms. You can see more of his work at olegvolk.net.

BONUS PHOTOS FROM HISTORY'S *TOP SHOT*

Photo of Ronnie Barrett and the author pictured with an M82A1 .50BMG rifle. Photo provided by author.

Chris posing with Battle Mug Joe and Iain Harrison.

Chris posing with two *Top Shot* fans at his September 2012 Bass Pro Shops appearances in Manteca, California. Photo courtesy of Bass Pro Shops.

While on the road between appearances, Chris visited the Jack Daniels factory in Tennessee and received a personalized bottle of Jack Daniels Single Barrel whiskey. Photo provided by author.

Chris teams up with YouTube Channel "The Legendary Shots" to perform trick shots using guns and basketballs. Photo courtesy of Samantha Hartsoe.

What makes *Top Shot* a great competition are the primitive weapons challenges. *Top Shot* Season 3 had to prove their marksmanship using knives, tomahawks, and one of man's first weapons: rocks. Photo courtesy of HISTORY.

The author's view of the *Top Shot* dueling tree challenge using an 1873 Winchester lever-action rifle.
Photo courtesy of HISTORY.

The *Top Shot* Season 4 Blue Team poses with *Top Shot* Season 2
Champion, Chris Reed, who was a shotgun expert that season.
Photo courtesy of HISTORY.

Top Shot is known for its creative and difficult challenges. Cliff Walsh, National Pistol Champion from *Top Shot* Season 3, navigates his way through a rolling ball challenge using a Glock 34 pistol, modified by Salient Arms International. Photo courtesy of HISTORY.

The author poses for a quick picture with the Red Team in triple digit heat while on the *Top Shot* range in Los Angeles, California. From left to right, front: Gary Shank, Gabby Franco. Rear: Danny "Chee" Kwan, Eric "Iggy" Keyes, Tim Trefren, and Kyle Sumpter. Photo courtesy of HISTORY.

George Reinas from *Top Shot* Season 2 takes out a 1,000 yard target in a single shot. Reinas is a sniper with the United States Air Force, and was a rifle expert on *Top Shot* Season 4. Photo courtesy of HISTORY.

The author's view of the *Top Shot* Season 4 final challenge where he used the Milkor M32A1 grenade launcher to blow up two platforms for the win. Photo courtesy of HISTORY.

The author poses with all the *Top Shot* Season 4 individual finalists immediately after winning the final challenge. From left to right: Augie Malekovich, Gary Shank, Gabby Franco, William Bethards, Danny "Chee" Kwan, Gregory Littlejohn, and Kyle Sumpter. Photo courtesy of HISTORY.

Top Shot host Colby Donaldson and Chris Reed take a break on the set of *Top Shot* Season 5 to pose with one of the competitor prizes, a pair of Oculus binoculars provided by Bass Pro Shops. Photo provided by author.

Chris Cheng poses with the *Top Shot* Season 5 "All-Stars" prize. A *Top Shot* customized Tahoe Q5i speedboat, provided by Bass Pro Shops. Photo provided by author.

All four *Top Shot* champions (Dustin Ellermann, Chris Cheng, Chris Reed, and Iain Harrison) posing with the "All Stars" sign while on the *Top Shot* range in Los Angeles, California. Photo provided by author.